Proust and Santayana

The Aesthetic Way of Life

PROUST *and*

SANTAYANA

THE AESTHETIC WAY OF LIFE

BY

VAN METER AMES

UNIVERSITY OF CINCINNATI

NEW YORK

RUSSELL & RUSSELL · INC

1964

TO MY WIFE

CONTENTS

AUTHOR'S NOTE

"New editions of books are a venture for publishers rather than for authors," Santayana said. "The author has committed his rash act once for all at the beginning and he can hardly retract or repeat it."[1] Yet afterthoughts on what has been said about Santayana are to be expected in his centennial year 1963. His detachment appeals to people too involved in doing; and charms others whose role is quieter; giving vicarious release to the heavy laden and some weight to those whose burden is light. All who believe in democracy, and still hope to make it work, must be distressed by his admiration of dictators. It may be explained as a spectator's overestimation of action he can only watch. But one too squeamish to sit through torture on the stage should be queasy about real brutality. Santayana survived enough war to want to abolish it and to hope for an ideal harmony of nations. He came to say that imperialism should be superseded,[2] though he did not see how the ideal could be attained except in contemplation.

What is at hand, as well as the unattainable, can be truly had only in its essence which is its "recognizable character...all of it that can actually be possessed in sensation or recovered in memory, or transcribed in art, or conveyed to another mind," he said in his essay on "Proust on Essences." There he was glad to recognize that Proust had discovered essences, but observed that Proust arrived at them through the recurrence of certain impressions, "as if essences needed to appear a second time in order to appear at all."[3] When he read the following book he objected to the contrast "of Proust's recovered experiences *with relations* as against my *unrelated* essences. An essence in both of us is identical with

[1]Preface to *Poems*, New York: Charles Scribner's Sons, 1923, p. vii.
[2]*Dominations and Powers*, Scribner's, 1951, p. 280.
[3]*Obiter Scripta*, Scribner's, 1936, pp. 273, 276.

itself no matter how often reconsidered: is identity a relation? ...Proust is weaving together *his memories*, whereas for me the dates and repetitions of intuitions are unimportant...His mind is autobiographical and novelesque: mine, even in my 'novel' is not, but rather moralistic, in the ancient sense of collecting insights, thoughts, and maxims. The *empirical* setting of these high lights interests me little in itself. Yet they, and every essence, has essential relations that define its character. It would not be true (or possible) that I consider essences apart from these internal or intrinsic relations. Besides, complex essences contain an arrangement of other essences accidental to the latter: so that the most complicated set of relations conceivable, if ever conceived, is intuited as one essence. The whole panorama of Proust's book, if one had mind enough, would thus appear absolutely and, if you like, unrelated."[4]

If Proust had read Santayana, there might have been an expression of surprise that such a disillusioned mind should retain the illusion of aristocracy, as if it ever was an ideal realized outside the realm of essence. And if Proust could have read this book he would have balked at the identification of him with his narrator. But now so much has been learned about both writers that what is said about them here is by way of illustrating the theme of contemplation, which is still worth presenting. Action continues to be needed, but the increase of leisure and of mass entertainment threatens to be demoralizing if aesthetic experience is not cultivated.

"Apology for Aesthetes" was published in *The International Journal of Ethics*, Vol. XLIV, No. 1, October, 1933. The quotations from the works of George Santayana are reprinted with the permission of Charles Scribner's Sons. For American readers the only versions of Proust are published by Random House and the Modern Library.

V.M.A.

Pentwater, Michigan
August, 1963

[4]Letter from Santayana, Rome, April 4, 1937, to the author; quoted in Van Meter Ames, *Zen and American Thought*, Honolulu: University of Hawaii Press, 1962, pp. 189-190.

I

Marcel Proust

MARCEL PROUST

Marcel Proust wrote to integrate and save himself, to give his life significance, to transmute the pain and bewilderment of a futile existence into art. Lacking the consolation of religious faith and finding science powerless to relieve his mental and physical suffering, he found comfort in the appreciation of art, and more in the practice of it when he metamorphosed from aesthete to artist, astonishing people who had regarded him as an idler and dilettante. He finally lived in a cork-lined room, stayed in bed most of the time, and could not go out in the warmest weather without an overcoat; he could not stand fresh air or sunshine — neither could he bear the exposure of his soul to any alien or indifferent influence from an impersonal universe, and had to make part of his inmost self all the worlds that had swum into his ken. *A la Recherche du Temps Perdu* is the record of his motivations, intentions and difficulties. As Mr. Middleton Murry has said, this novel is a commentary on itself, written to explain itself. Yet in affirming his experience Proust achieved more than he dreamed, for in pouring his own spirit into literature he expressed his age.

The leisurely length of the great work enabled it to acquire a momentum and ultimately a velocity that nothing could stop. The accumulated difficulties of matter and form and execution were exploded by their own force as Proust sifted the significance from gross

3

experience and released the energy locked in minutiae. With the interferometer of his intelligence he measured to the millionth of an inch the spectra filtered by his intuition; with data fantastically infinitesimal his imagination skyrocketed over distances astronomical; and the too-solid stuff of common sense melted into mystery and starlight.

For several volumes he seems merely to be recalling his past with prolixity of perception and subtlety of analysis. He is apparently writing down everything he can remember, and one may feel that this is enough, so satisfying is the result. Perhaps the importance of form in art has been overrated, or it may be that the form of life will do for art. Instead of mastering his subject matter and compelling it to a pattern, it may be sufficient for the writer to submit to his material and follow the vague configuration it happens to have.

Proust shows that the interweaving pathways of association have naturally a structure not different from the organization characterizing art. Since artistic form is an arrangement of pleasing repetition, to trace in retrospect pleasure-giving recurrences will shape a work of art. Every kind of art supplies the counterpart of a past in its formal relationships, and to enjoy them is like indulging in reminiscence, so that for Proust to recall his past was not for him to forget the importance of form, but to find ready at hand forms worked out and worn smooth by the course of his own life.

He has been accused of inability to control his material only by readers too short-winded to follow him through. In addition to the form he found in life, he deliberately devised integration and equilibrium, so that the reader who continues gradually realizes that beneath the fine texture of Proust's novel is a powerful articulation; that interesting as the details are in themselves there is more interest in their reference; that great as his achievement would remain if it were merely the autobiography it first appears to be, it is infinitely greater when seen to have the architectonic that has always ribbed and vaulted a consummate work of art. Admiring the tensile strength of this vast structure, the reader may even feel that it is too tightly riveted; the wonder of seeing joined together things that had been kept asunder may verge on the suspicion that it has been overdone. In the last volumes the various themes are caught up and blended until the conclusion rolls in with the force and finality of an orchestra coasting to the close of a symphony.

Persons who appear too briefly to be noticed except in passing, like M. de Charlus and Rachel *Quand du Seigneur*, return as important characters. Casual remarks flicked off like the ashes of a cigarette flare up in a conflagration of consequences; trivial incidents turn out to be hinges of the whole. Nothing stands still, everything shifts and moves on, falls and shoots up again. As plants bend toward the sun, all things incline toward the past, the source of all that follows and the illumination of every dark place, as it slowly comes up in the revolution of the novel. The end approaches with the acceleration of a planet nearing the perihelion, as the past suddenly appears ahead when the orbit is nearly completed. At the close, Proust is gathering speed to swing into the beginning, he is getting ready to write the book he has written; and the reader is swept around to the first volume, but with a sense of complete resolution.

Proust wishes to avoid factitious symmetry, but seems obliged to exaggerate unity in his novel to show that

unity in life cannot be exaggerated. He wants the ultimate unity that Balzac discovered among pieces needing
only to be brought together; not an artificial, forced
unity, but the kind that is not seen at first, " hence vital
and not logical, which has not shut out variety and
frozen execution " (*La Prisonnière*, I, 219). So the
unity of his work dovetails with his associations which
he said were so crisscrossed that he had a great choice of
paths from one point to another. Everything in his experience is tied up, through an elaborate exchange, with
everything else. After the marriage of the obscure and
the brilliant, the upstart and the established, a time comes
when nothing has more significance or higher rank than
anything else, when even Swann's Way and the Guermantes Way are one. So it was as profitable for Proust
to have spent his hours with a frivolous girl like Albertine
as with a man of genius like Elstir. " After a certain age
our memories are so interwoven that the thing we are
thinking of, the book we are reading has almost no importance left. We have scattered something of ourselves
everywhere, everything is fecund, everything is dangerous, and the discoveries we can make in the *Pensées* of
Pascal are not more precious than those we can make in
an advertisement for soap " (*Albertine Disparue*, I, 203).
Proust had unraveled something of himself at every step
of his development, and could not rest until he had gath-
ered up the skein of his past to wind it close in the lap of
his consciousness.

His material was all one, and he naturally said that a
novelist has only one novel (*La Prisonnière*, II, 235).
He could not have written more than one, no matter
how long it had to be, because the world to be included
was one and indivisible. He tried to avoid chapter divi-

sions; he put off paragraph indentations indefinitely; he hated to finish a sentence; because all that he wanted to say was dissolved in the same solution and had to be poured out at once.

He believed that an artist does not create through knowledge but through the ability to put away learning unabsorbed in unconscious processes, and illustrated this belief in the character of Elstir. He had "an exceptionally cultivated intelligence," as shown by his discourse on the Balbec church, but before painting he would "in the presence of reality despoil himself of all the notions of his intelligence," would make himself ignorant, would forget everything through utter honesty (*Jeunes Filles*, III, 105). Proust himself never succeeded for long in dispensing with the intellect, but intended for it to be added sparingly to instinct and intuition, which means that he wanted to subordinate technique to vision. "It is not the most intellectual or the best informed of men . . . but he who knows how to make himself a mirror and can reflect his life, even though it is mediocre, who becomes a Bergotte" (*Le Temps Retrouvé*, I, 41).

When the narrator entered Elstir's studio it seemed to him "like a laboratory for a sort of new creation of the world" (*Jeunes Filles*, III, 97). Of the various studies there he said: "I could discern that the charm of each consisted in a kind of metamorphosis of the things represented, analogous to what in poetry is called metaphor, and that if God the Father had created things in naming them, it was through taking away their names, or in naming them anew that Elstir recreated them" (*Jeunes Filles*, III, 98). Proust might have been a painter himself, so sensitive were his analyses of composition, and so observant was he of the elements of painting in the world around him after Elstir had opened his eyes — as in the harmonies of shape and color in objects on the table after a meal (Cf. *Jeunes Filles*, III, 144, 145).

Elstir and the author both mirrored the reality around them, but always with the refraction of their genius. Each relied upon the spontaneous play of relatively unconscious and automatic abilities, and laid aside until an opportune moment the more unwieldy machinery of reflection. But when Proust had his intuitions in hand he analyzed them pitilessly, for he tried to be as realistic as he was romantic. His protracted analyses were as much his own, however, and as deeply dyed with his unique personality as his immediate insights. Truth was his aim as well as beauty, but he believed each artist found beauty in a special world of his own, and said: " Only through art can we go out of ourselves to know what another sees of a universe which is not the same as ours and whose scenery would otherwise have remained as unknown as what there may be on the moon " (*Le Temps Retrouvé*, II, 49).

Proust felt that deep in his subconscious self was a book that could not be read off by the intelligence, that had to be slowly deciphered by a procedure he called creation, though the authenticity of what was brought to light was attested by the fact of his not being free to choose it, because it was simply given (Cf. *Le Temps Retrouvé*, II, 25). He would have agreed with Croce that creativity precedes the reflective level where choice takes place. " The duty and the task of a writer are those of a translator " (*Le Temps Retrouvé*, II, 41). The important thing is that out of his creative copying Proust achieved a novel. He himself became impatient with the difficulty of explaining how it happened, and declared in the midst of his theorizing that true art accomplishes itself in silence; that while it is a great temptation to write intellectual works, it is a great indelicacy, because a work with theories in it is like an object with the price tag on it (*Le Temps Retrouvé*, II, 29).

His whole story was implicit in the early impressions of the little boy at Combray, a place not on the map of France but in his imagination (*Le Temps Retrouvé*, II, 130). What others regarded as reality was alien to him. He was happy only in reading and dreaming and hoping to become a writer, except for his mother's kiss and for moments when something he contemplated became filled with mystery like the steeples of Martinville. Not by deliberate intellectual recall but through a Bergsonian process of unconscious memory, which first dawned on him in the case of the little cakes dipped in tea, whereby something in the present opened a breach in oblivion to let the past flood in and overflow the living moment, Proust acquired material inherently imaginative and charged with emotion, needing only to be concentrated to become a work of art. For him the power of art, like the spell of remembrance and the force of childhood premonitions, rested upon the revelation of identities between the present and the past. So he undertook to trace out faithfully the ties between his sensations and memories, his maturity and his childhood, and to write down the abiding essences of his life as they were already written in the inner book of his being.

Though it would seem *a priori* that art might take flight from the present or the future as well as from the past, and though Proust believed that forms and meanings in art partake of the eternal, it was in retrospect that he gained access to them. It was on the horizon of memory that his heaven touched his earth, except for rare moments when a Jacob's ladder of insight was let down to him directly. Usually he found the present unfertile unless irrigated by the past. He was not wistful about the earlier years of his existence or previous eras of history for their own sake, but because the thought of them stimulated his imagination and enabled him to rise from the real to the ideal — not merely from the present to the past, from the living to the dead, but from life to art.

He said that " life not yet lived, life relatively future, seems to us a life more distant, more detached, less useful, less ours " than days we have already had (*La Prisonnière*, I, 131). He was drawn to the past because its remoteness gave it the psychic distance of a work of art on its pedestal or in its frame. He may have meant that the future is relatively unfurnished with imagery of intimate concern, and in that sense " less ours " and " less useful," because less conducive to the joy of contemplation. Yet the future was not empty to him; he saw contingencies arising and felt the painful necessity of making plans.

It is a temptation to say that for Proust the present was neutral in tone, the future anxious, and the past delightful. This was the tendency of his consciousness; but there were two shattering exceptions: Albertine and Venice. Albertine, day after day, through her presence and her absence, through what she did and refrained from doing, through what she revealed and hid, stretched the immediate moment into an eternity of hours cut off from before and after, during which she exposed him to a scale of suffering, from uneasiness to torture, or to a treacherous enjoyment ranging from relief to ecstasy.

She also poisoned the well of the past, for he never knew when a fresh aspect of her career would transpire to put him on the rack. There was one Albertine in the past whom he loved to think of, but there were a hundred others. Albertine made him face about and long for the future when he might be rid of her and escape to Venice where he had never been. Often the spell of the past in the music of Vinteuil died away while the barcarole of the gondoliers came floating across the lagoons of anticipation, and he turned from the memory of old impressions to an old desire (*La Prisonnière*, II, 283, 284).

But whether looking backward or forward, Proust loved to contemplate the pervasive qualities in his experience, the essences of things withdrawn from time (*Le Temps Retrouvé*, II, 40). Much like Santayana, Proust thought of essences as subsisting eternally, independent of generation and decay, possessing no efficacy, but offering in themselves, to anyone able to appreciate them, the satisfaction that otherwise eluded him in life, in love or travel. In all his questing his unhappiness had been relieved only by art, a few memories, and certain impressions which had immediately struck him as concealing a transcendent truth. Comparing these three kinds of happy experience he found that they were alike in removing all anxiety, including the fear of death, because during them he became an extra-temporal being absorbed in essences (*Le Temps Retrouvé*, II, 14).

The calm of the "eternal man," however, did not quell the passion of the man of letters. Insouciance induced by contemplation of essences whetted his desire to write. Yet there was no contradiction, because writing was to him the most effective means of cleaving to the eternity in essences. Writing was the exercise and

discipline through which he reached his mystical fulfillment. Throughout his life, after he had once discovered
his real orientation, the future was the opportunity to
write; the past was something to write about. When
Albertine ceased to trouble him, when Venice was
pigeon-holed in memory between Combray and Balbec,
when there was nothing else to live for, the taut bow of
his book still was aimed ahead.

Despite the importance he attributed to impressions
outside time, he realized that they would not fill a book,
and a book he must have to conquer time. So among the
verities of extra-temporal experience he included truths
dependent on time: " Time in which men, societies, nations, bathe and change " (*Le Temps Retrouvé*, II, 101).
And to read Proust is to live through genuine durations
with his characters as they alter with the years. None
of them resists age; each continues to change, through
what time adds and through what it progressively reveals. Like the hour hand Proust's novel apparently
stands still while he devotes hundreds of pages to one
day, one dinner; but before long — just long enough to
read a book — the fullness of a lifetime has ticked away,
and one life after another has ended. " Life is like a
pantomime in which one sees from act to act the baby
become adolescent, the mature man bend over to the
tomb " (*Le Temps Retrouvé*, II, 91).

It was not the timeless but Time that was the fitting
subject and the close of a work inspired by insight into
eternal essences. Yet this concern with time is not surprising, since all who have discoursed upon ultimate
being have done so by contrasting it with becoming.
And if philosophers have flirted with paradox, incon-
sistency should not be held against a romancer who ri-

valed the *Arabian Nights*. Proust's novel might not
suffer if it were not the logical result and continuation
of his metaphysical speculation, as he thought. Yet no
logic could lead more directly to the bourne beyond
time than his relentless rendering of time.

The truth, as he saw it, was forced on him in his effort
to reconcile himself to his fate. He felt that his suffering
was an instance of the temporal lot, and that it could be
surmounted not by the literal satisfaction of desire, but
through imaginative fulfillment in contemplation of
values picked out by the searchlight of longing. So he
said that it is better to want something than to get it;
that " poverty is more generous than opulence " (*La
Prisonnière*, I, 83). He pitied anyone who could jump
into a carriage and drive straight to the realization of his
dream. Only after wandering forty years in the desert
of disillusion was Proust able to escape from the Egypt
of existence to the Canaan of essence.

In coming to regard the experience of evil as the highest good he revealed how he was goaded, how he was
forced to interpret his life in a light that he could bear
and that would enable him to carry out his literary ambition, which was his only road to peace. He determined
to find in his very misery the power to achieve his salvation. He saw that, just as it was, his life had been unconsciously a preparation for literature; that his magazine of
grief, the dry powder of his whole past, was ready to
burst into flame. Having discovered in the pit of despair
the means of escape from futility, if not from loneliness,
he scorned hedonism and declared happiness to have
only one use, that of making unhappiness possible.
" The writer may undertake a long task without fear.
If intelligence begins the work, along the way a host of

sorrows will appear to see it through " (*Le Temps Re-trouvé*, II, 65). With the winning of this conviction he laid aside everything that had hindered him, or turned it to advantage. He had wasted his life and was sick. But, " as laziness had saved him from facility, so his malady would keep him from laziness," for he knew his time was short (*Le Temps Retrouvé*, II, 258).

Through the narration of his unhappiness he discerned in it more clearly the rhythms and relationships that had soothed him in reminiscence and other aesthetic experience. Unhealthy, unhappy, unsuccessful, he sought strength, joy and achievement, and found them in his sorrow itself when he raised it to art. On account of his disillusionment, and not in spite of it, he reveled in imagination. If he saw gods and goddesses about him, it was not because they had left Olympus to dwell on earth, but because there was no one on earth to comfort him, and he could not stand his loneliness without ideal company.

Of the many evils to which he had to reconcile himself, the worst was the death of his grandmother, who was the personification of all values located in his past. After her lingering death he found no substitute for her in the women whose beautiful names decorated the succeeding epochs of his life: Odette, Gilberte, Oriane and Albertine. Finally time carried away even the vivid memory of his grandmother.

Her place was taken after a fashion by Albertine, but the anguish she caused him confirmed him in the belief that love is entirely subjective, that it is impossible to know the beloved, and perhaps better not to. The lies which entangled his relation with Albertine were a travesty on the mutual confidence he had yearned for. " As a child I had dreamed that the sweetest thing in love, its very essence, was to pour out freely, before the one I loved, my tenderness, my gratitude for her kindness, my desire for a perpetual life in common. But too soon I learned from my own experience and from that of my friends that the expression of such sentiments is far from being contagious " (*La Prisonnière*, II, 196).

His love degenerated into jealousy. He was suspicious of Albertine in all her relations with people, not only because she was no better than she should be, but because every hour she spent with someone else forever thwarted his efforts to imagine her at one with him. He did not love her for herself, because whenever he momentarily felt sure of her he was bored and hoped she would go away, never to come back and trouble him again. He saw her as a bar across his path: she kept him from other women and from the alluring journey to Venice. But as soon as she was out of sight his suspicions made him ache for her, made him forgive everything, and he was ready to marry her and pour out his fortune for her. It was when she made him jealous that he loved her with a raging despair. Then he thought of her as she had first appeared on the beach, against the great back-drop of the sea, when her personality was still a blank to be filled in by his imagination. The discrepancy between the initial Albertine, sealed within his impression of her, and the ramifying traces of her life apart from him, was irreducible except while she was asleep, when her personality again was in abeyance and he could yearn over her without anxiety. The better he knew her the more inaccessible and recalcitrant she seemed, because he became ever more aware of her hidden selves contradicting or threatening to overthrow his wishful version of her.

Yet any inference was so unreliable that perhaps he
wronged her, and it might even be that she loved him.
He was immensely proud of her intellectual development under his influence and thought he might take this
as evidence of her affection; but he was so distrustful of
anything outside himself, so accustomed to attribute any
satisfaction to his inner activity, that he could never believe anyone really loved him, except his mother and
grandmother. He tortured himself in continually seeking out Albertine's guilt, though to spare himself he had
to doubt or discount the most incriminating evidence.
If only he could get rid of her or assimilate her, he
thought he might find peace. But, like the *jinn* escaped
from the bottle, Albertine, in the nightmare proportions
of Proust's jealousy, could not be forced back into the
shape she had once had on the beach.

He believed that love was subjective, that it would
have been the same for him if he had not known Albertine. The real evil to which he had to become reconciled in life and love was the fact of being himself. He
noted the futility of conjecturing what his life would
have been had it been different, because his imagination
was conditioned by his past. Since he was himself he
felt that all his adventures were bound to be variations
on the same theme. Not only were his love affairs alike,
but in each of them the whole development was implicit
in the beginning. The eagerness with which he had
longed to meet Albertine while she was inaccessible, and
the perversity with which he lost interest in her when a
meeting seemed easy, foreshadowed his entire relation
with her and summed up his vicissitudes with other
women. In Albertine he was not choosing to worship
the opposite of all he admired — for to him she was fate,

irreversible time, the present that could be only a mockery of the past. Whatever one thinks of her (and one
may take her side) it is plain that even had she possessed
all the virtues he would have been incapable of prolonged
happiness with her, for her vice was innocent and wholesome compared with his morbid inability to value anything but the unattainable.

He pathetically treasured any sign that the objective
order was friendly to him, yet could not believe that an
apparent kindness had any reality outside his imagination.
While he discounted favors from without, he had no
difficulty in crediting external agents with the power to
plague him at every turn; though he might have regarded
this as simply the weakness of his imaginative strength,
for his own illusions exposed him to disillusion. He soon
realized that his sorry scheme of keeping Albertine under
surveillance was doomed to failure because it violated his
code of coping with evil through inner activity. His attempt to step out of himself and control the intransigeant
universe in its own terms was a mistake, because the
outer order seemed to oppose him and threaten his arrest
at every point. He held Albertine captive, but knew
himself a prisoner in the solitary confinement of his own
consciousness.

His despair of fidelity in Albertine rested upon the
conviction of fickleness in himself. Similarly he felt that
the faults of Françoise were the counterpart of his own
qualities, so that nothing would have been gained by dismissing her and hiring another servant. The illiterate
old peasant woman matched his psychological complexity. Swann, Saint-Loup, the Baron, though each was
decidedly an individual, were all mirrors of the narrator;
they shared his hypersensitiveness and introversion, and

their sentimental adventures were parodies when not duplicates of his own. Morel was of the same stripe, though more unbalanced; Elstir and Bergotte were the same, though more sane. An entire society, with its heaving strata and disappearing individuals, Proust conjured out of himself. Over its ample area his own seething experience was projected: there his desires, disappointments and entanglements were spread out and magnified. He even saw international relations as a grotesque enlargement of his affair with Albertine.

But it was easier for him to reconcile himself to his own perversity than to the vanity around him. Amid the glitter of society Proust, who came to worship with the wonder of a young bourgeois, remained to scoff with the wrath of a Hebrew prophet. Distinctions which the world made much of, he learned to the least detail, first through adoration and then through vindictiveness. He was fascinated by characteristics separating social levels and believed (almost superstitiously) that they could be sensed even when objectively invisible. But he learned to look on with the unprejudiced eye of an artist, equally interested in all the forms and colors of life, awake to the values of the individual as well as to those of the species. His great repertory of figures are living human beings because they are all individualized, each standing on his own feet without ever being sheltered from analysis or unfairly lighted on account of belonging to a type. The Duchess of Guermantes is revealed in her merits and her faults exactly like the old servant Françoise. No advocate of a classless society could be more contemptuous of class distinctions as indexes of personal worth than Proust.

The worldliness he despised was chiefly a feminine

affair. It is the women in his novel who organize the salons, are responsible for them, and take them seriously. With the exception of the effeminate Baron, the men come just to amuse themselves or to humor the ladies. The men always have something more important on their minds — usually love. Homosexuality makes no difference but for convention, and that is the point of Proust's exhaustive treatment of this subject as he developed its comic, pathetic and lurid aspects. Yet it was not a matter of indifference to him whether he represented men or women, for he took a very masculine (and French) view of woman: if she was attractive she was a courtesan, as deceiving as alluring.

To him men are the real lovers because women are capable of caring deeply only for fashion and social standing. It is the men who are sensitive and suffering in love, who are idealistic and deceived. The women come through it relatively unaffected. Odette, Albertine and Rachel are serene in contrast to the havoc they cause as objects of love, though it is hinted that Albertine suffers. Oriane and Gilberte do not seem ruffled by their marital difficulties, and the unhappiness of Jupien's jilted daughter is not made very serious compared to the heartaches of men like Swann, the Baron and the narrator — though her fiancé, the violinist, seems to have no feeling except for his art.

The female of the Proustian species equals the male in depth of emotion only when engaged in rivalry for social prestige. Then she is fully aroused, she schemes and woos like a lover. She suffers the pangs of jealousy in defeat, like Mme. de Ste. Euverte; and after the flush of success she becomes indifferent to it until she has lost it, like Mme. de Villeparisis who holds on to a brilliant remnant of her former position in the person of Mme. de Guermantes — who in turn becomes bored with her own unquestioned pre-eminence and loses her hold in the same way. Meanwhile in an epic struggle Mme. Verdurin fights all the way up from the bottom. But if love is subjective, what difference does it make if the women focus their emotion on social success? And if women are inferior, to fall in love with them is hardly a sign of superiority in men; while no lovers are more miserably duped than the homosexuals of both sexes. Despicable as society is represented to be, it is scarcely a poorer outlet for emotion than the experience of lovers known to Proust.

Disillusioned by the life around him, he asked himself whether there was nothing else, nothing more real, more worthy of his idealism and loyalty. He saw morality as a mockery and religion as a sloughed-off folkway, nor had science any ultimate validity for him. There was no redemptive power in politics; business he did not even consider as an occupation, much less as a salvation. In none of the professions did he see any virtue beyond that of a trade by which to make a living. One might be a great doctor or a famous professor and still be an ass like Cottard or a bore like Brichot.

But hard as it was for Proust to reconcile himself to his own character and to existence, what most disturbed him in himself and in the world was the fact of change. He was always trying to retrace his steps to recover what had been left behind. He could not ignore the fear, later borne out, that his great love for Albertine would suffer the same diminution and final disappearance as his earlier devotion to Gilberte or Mme. de Guermantes — like Swann's love for Odette — and that he would forget

Albertine as completely and unregretfully as his grandmother. Everyone dies, everything passes. Successive
selves, carrying on the fiction of the same personality,
vanish every few years, so that Proust could say he was
no longer the man who had loved Albertine, but had
only heard her talked about. He knew that if she were
to come back after her last disappearance she would not
be the same and neither would he. Should she write to
say there had been a mistake, that she was still alive, he
would not answer the letter. Every nuance of losing
and remembering her, and slowly surrendering her to
oblivion, he recorded in what are among his most beautiful pages, along with the contradictions in the hope of a
heavenly reunion, with the moral that each person is indeed alone. The temporal man is an unremaining phantom and the things he reaches for have no substance.

Proust sought relief in exchanging the present for the
past, or the future. He often wanted to break away
from Albertine to follow a woman glimpsed in passing,
whose charm inhered in being unknown, as he had moods
in which the unvisited city of dreams beckoned him
more than the sacred places of memory. But he had no
sooner arrived in Venice than it reminded him of Combray. His life was an illustration of Schopenhauer's
restless, tormented Will, always striving for something
absent. And like Schopenhauer, Proust found comfort
in the art of writing, perhaps more than in identification
with " the eternal man " and the essence of things.

The more meanly he thought of himself and the way
he had wasted his life, the more he hoped to make up for
lost time by the use of his literary gifts. He was encour-
aged by what Elstir the painter said: " There is no wise
man who at some time in his youth has not pronounced

words, or even led an existence the memory of which is disagreeable to him and which he would like to wipe out. But he should not altogether regret it, because he cannot be sure of having become wise, in the degree that is possible, unless he has passed through all the ridiculous or odious incarnations which must precede that last incarnation " (*Jeunes Filles*, III, 137). Proust had always felt himself to be potentially a writer; his grandmother had fully expected him to become one, and he was greatly chagrined to have disappointed her. Albertine was convinced that sheer laziness kept him from writing. Bergotte had highly praised his early essays. Much as his loyalties wavered or weakened, Proust's passion for art and especially for literature never waned. But he thought it was an unrequited love and had long resigned himself to passive appreciation when he realized with overpowering emotion that literary success might be his.

It is difficult to say which is more to be admired, the fidelity with which Proust revealed life or the completeness with which he transmuted it into art. Only in life could there be such fullness, depth and authenticity; only in art such selection and form. His book must have been his own experience, yet it must have been invented. He was naturalistic and profoundly disillusioned, but also romantic. His heroines have more than feet of clay; some of his heroes might be mistaken for villains; the society in which they move is vain. But what seemed a pit of despair became a hill of hope.

In imaginative remembrance and artistic re-creation of the past the pain and triviality of life acquired the value of art: they ceased to be sordid to become exalting, to be shaken by a tremor of significance that redeemed evil — not to make it good but purifyingly bad, as it could be only in imagination. What enjoyment Proust had formerly found in life had come to him chiefly from works of art, and rare moments like the experience of the three trees, in which existence, taking on the spell of art, had tinctured his sea of troubles with drops of redeeming blood. So he vowed to pour his whole past into art, what was already beautiful along with what was not. Having observed that subject-matter was indifferent to a painter who could make a masterpiece out of a shack or out of a cathedral already a work of art, Proust took the stupidity and pettiness, the vice, folly and cruelty of his friends, as well as their noble qualities; he took the perversity and vanity of his own life, the desperate loneliness of it; he took the anguish of his mind and body, with the moments of bliss, and through the alchemy of art left nothing but beauty.

His life had fallen far short of art until he became an artist. Only then did his early misery (and occasional joy) become a lost paradise to be regained through the remembrance of things past. He transmuted his life without recourse to mythology or religion, except for the sake of metaphor; and he resorted to figures of speech not to bedeck his memoirs but because only through allegory and allusion could he express the emotion he felt when anything floated back to him across the vista of the years. Change, the destroyer, when overtaken by the wings of imagination, became like the illusion of movement in an arabesque, ever returning in an eternal pattern.

His grandmother had died, but in his imagination " death, like a sculptor of the Middle Ages, laid her in the form of a young maiden," and she came back more precious and present for having been lost. Albertine

became again as he had first seen her. The suffering she
had caused him now burned away its absurdity in a new
intensity that made unspeakably soothing the " daily
bread " of her endearments. Odette regained the Botti-
celli look that made Swann love her; Gilberte smiled
with the knowledge that Proust had at last discovered
her love for him; and his mother would never again fail
to kiss him good-night. He rescued them all from the
past and created them anew, along with the terrible and
wonderful Françoise, the incomparable friend Saint-
Loup, the Verdurins, La Berma, Elstir, Bergotte, and the
unbelievable Baron Charlus — with their deeds, their
talk and gestures, their very thoughts. Around this
world of people, living a new and endless life, Proust
wrought a frieze of lovely working girls; above he set
the steeple of St. Hilaire; throughout he wove the music
of Vinteuil.

He hoped that his work might be a fulfillment of the
lives of his grandmother and others. With the glow of
the artist who feels that he has at long last risen above the
aesthete, he triumphed tenderly over Swann: " Dear
Charles Swann, whom I knew when I was still young
and you were near the grave, it is because he whom you
must have thought a little imbecile has made you a hero
of one of his romances, that people begin again to speak
of you and that perhaps you will live " (*La Prisonnière*,
I, 273). Since those whom Proust had loved most had
in the course of time become incomprehensible words
to him, he said: " If there is a way of learning to understand these forgotten words, ought we not to use that
means, which, though it would be universal, would at
least be permanent, which would make of those who are
no more, in their truest essence, a perpetual acquisition

for all souls? And that law of change which has ren-
dered these words unintelligible to us — if we succeed in
explaining it, will not our inferiority become a new
strength? Moreover, the work in which our troubles
have collaborated may be interpreted in the future as at
once a nefarious sign of suffering and a happy sign of
consolation " (*Le Temps Retrouvé*, II, 60). So he
found comfort in transferring himself and his friends to
a world of art removed from actual existence with its
arbitrary entrances and exits.

Had he written before the French Revolution, when
the aristocrats whose names emboss his pages had the
lands, the rights and obligations that their titles boast,
their nobility would have been a matter of fact without
the anachronistic charm of lingering in a modern re-
public; their arms, colored still with the pale tints of
actuality, might never have blazed with the heraldry
of Proust's imagination; their pride, in being justified,
would have been less poetic; their complex hierarchical
relationships and inflexible rules of precedence, in having some importance, would not have had the purely
formal and symbolic beauty of a tapestry. When the
Guermantes had " the right of life and death over their
vassals," before the age of Charlemagne, they had not
yet received the fealty of art.

The aristocracy had the same interest for Proust as
the old church at Balbec. The centuries had brought
decay and restoration, altering or effacing details, but
leaving the old forms with their associations; and the
vestiges of feudalism, without temporal or spiritual
power, had an aesthetic authority like that of any forms
or meanings which have a lasting hold on the imagination
— in contrast to the ephemeral coercion of mere exist-

ence. The Guermantes, though deprived of economic or political excuse for their position, had the same claim to respect as the Musée de Cluny with its relics of the Crusades, the Panthéon with its roll of glory, or the Louvre and the Bibliothèque Nationale with their treasures of the past.

By a trick of inversion Proust identified the idle *élite* with the tillers of the soil. The value he attached to the aristocracy he often attributed to an earthy, peasant quality, to a local sap and pith in their conversation, savoring of the " *rapprochements* between the chateau and the village " (*La Prisonnière*, I, 44–46). He praised Mme. de Guermantes for being aware of this aspect of her charm and maintained that no false simplicity was involved. It was not a question of the powdered shepherds and shepherdesses of Louis XVI's court. But neither was it really the autocthonous character of the nobility, their long contact with the land and peasantry, which fascinated Proust so much as their daily use of expressions that reminded him of literature. He listened to Mme. de Guermantes as he would read " a book written in a language of former times," with " that pure French grace which one does not find any more, either in speech or writing." And he had the same pleasure in hearing Françoise, for she also delighted him with an archaic vocabulary and what he felt to be the true pronunciation of words — until she was corrupted by her daughter and the steward. The talk of both the duchess and the servant wafted the past to him.

Everything which interested him became other than its prosaic self. All life's furnishings and fixtures, vehicles and devices, he slipped from the gigantic dust cover hiding their brightness. Automobiles and airplanes became as wondrous as the stage coaches of Dickens or the chariots of Homer. Maids, waiters and elevator boys acquired an epic quality. The cries of street vendors became a symphony. The butcher boy with his dazzling scales became an Angel of Judgment, separating and weighing souls. Proust's first encounter with an airplane was an almost mythological experience, and he went with Albertine to the airport to watch the planes landing and leaving as he took her to a museum or a church before dinner. He enjoyed riding in automobiles, but without any thought of how they were made or their sociological import. He reveled in the experience like a child on a circus elephant and told about it like Marco Polo describing a curiosity of Cathay. The machine was like a magic carpet. To him the chauffeur did not manipulate a mechanism through knowledge of cause and effect, but was like an apostolic figure on a cathedral porch or in a stained glass window, his hand resting on the steering wheel " as on a cross of consecration " (*La Prisonnière*, I ,182). And the animistic attitude Proust took toward the telephone and the impersonal demoiselles of the exchange whom he tried to personify, became sheer poetry.

With all his lore and psychological penetration, his metaphysical ability and training, he was like a sage from the remote past somehow living in modern Paris, for whom science other than the ancient literary sort was magic not worth trying to understand. He simply added the inventions of science to the wonders of nature and art, as part of the universal spectacle for contemplation. The only value of science to him was the material and vocabulary it provided for his unscientific imagination. He was convinced that medicine, which is the most immediate application of science to human ills, only aggravated his own. He made much of observation, experiment and verification, but his method was intuitive and personal rather than objective and co-operative. His procedure had nothing in common with laboratory research or library scholarship, with field work or case work. For him science was a mine of symbols with which to create art. All the paraphernalia of culture had value for him only in becoming part of his own experience and enabling him to cast it in art. Knowledge was of no use except as it helped him to know himself, and he was not content with any extant expression because he cared for it only as it could symbolize what he felt, and only an art springing directly from his own life could adequately express his feeling.

His life was so restricted externally that vast tracts of the modern scene he never saw at all — which is partly the reason why his novel takes the reader away from dull reality as much as Arabian tales. Business does not exist in his pages except for its ancient form surviving in a picturesque fringe of small shopkeepers and street-hawkers. He ignored the industrial revolution. The world's work was done off the stage of his consciousness, though suggested by a few colored sets, the occasional appearance of a laborer, and now and then by a chorus that must represent the masses. In the whole gallery of major and minor characters there is not a single portrait of a business man (unless Jupien is one); Bloch's scarcely mentioned uncle is the only banker; there is not an engineer, priest, salesman, factory worker, miner or sailor, and only a suggestion of a farmer. No one but M. de Crécy is really in need of money, though Professor Brichot uses street cars and the Reine de Naples is in

straitened circumstances.   Economic unrest is not
hinted. The great repertory is practically limited to the
leisure class and their retainers who share the same
values.

The whole spectacle of which Proust was aware might
have been recorded practically intact had he lived centuries earlier. Some motives and decorative schemes
would have been missing. There would have been no
elevators, automobiles or telephones, but that would not
have mattered to Proust any more than to Diaghilev,
who, in planning a ballet, could achieve the same success
in adapting and stylizing the surfaces of today or yester-
day; or to Diego Rivera, who painted murals with the
forms and rhythms of rural Mexico and then covered
walls with equally compelling patterns taken from the
machines and processes of American industry. Like any
artist, Proust worked with the materials familiar to him;
and the way he wove in everything he saw, regardless of
what it was, shows that subject matter was indifferent to
him as long as he could fit it in through similarity or contrast, to heighten an effect he already had in mind, or to
make another that he had not thought of before.

The good he won from existence he might have
achieved in the Middle Ages or in ancient Greece, if he
could have been himself; for what he valued was his own
way of seeing and associating things. Yet alien as he
was to the age he lived in, his orchid-like consciousness
could have flowered only in the hot-house atmosphere
of modern aestheticism, glassed in by the class distinctions which fascinated him, planted in soil enriched by
all previous culture, and watered by the inspiration of
recent or contemporary civilization. Without Greek
art and mythology; without the smoldering memory of

Sodom and Gomorrah; without medieval monuments and ideologies already archaic; without Venice; without Saint-Simon, Racine, Balzac, Dostoievsky and Ruskin — without Bergson — Proust's mode of seeing and feeling would have been impossible; nor could his sensibility have preceded modern music and painting. He is inconceivable without his personal and cultural past, the recovery of which was his art.

Art for him was not merely emotional fireworks, not simply complicated play, but the most earnest concern of man, the only one that could save him from futility. He was so pessimistic about existence in general and enthusiastic about art in particular that he was unwilling to call art the best part of life — it was too good for life. Among all the blind alleys he saw, art was the only avenue leading through to the open country of hope. Anything not art, or not redeemed by a touch of art, was death — though he called it life. Merely to be alive was already to be dead; to embrace art was to escape life and to triumph over death.

But though he often asserted this faith in art, he had his doubts. " Was there in art a deeper reality in which our true personality finds an expression that the activities of life do not give? " Perhaps art was not worth sacrificing for, perhaps it was not " something from beyond life, not sharing its vanity and nothingness . . ." (*La Prisonnière*, I, 270). He was afraid that the originality of great artists, instead of being the reflection of a reality more than human, might be only the result of industry and technical cleverness.

In thinking about the death of Bergotte and in meditating on Vinteuil's *Septet*, Proust swung back to the feeling that in art was a " formula eternally true, forever

fecund with an unknown joy, a mystic hope." He
sensed " the strange call which henceforth I should never
cease to hear, as the promise and proof that something
else existed, attainable through art . . . besides the void
which I had found in all my pleasures and even in love,
and that if my life had seemed vain, at least it had not exhausted everything " (*La Prisonnière*, II, 82). This
may be taken as his final view, since it appears in the volume he was working on at the last. In fact he is said to
have rewritten the passage about Bergotte's death as his
own approached, and he could not bring himself to believe that Bergotte was gone forever. Somehow his
achievement must save him even after the freezing of
the planet.

In discussing his mystical interpretation of art, Proust
said that we seem to enter this life with a burden of obligations contracted in a previous existence, and that this
explains the urge to art (*La Prisonnière*, I, 255, 256).
He would not say that art saves man by giving stimulus
and outlet to his imagination, an opportunity for him to
integrate himself through contemplation of form and
rhythm, and a chance to feel equal to the world through
finding his problems solved symbolically. He would
not admit that art provides simply an intensification of
consciousness. This would not do for Proust, at least
when he believed art to be an intimation of immortality.
He interpreted the feeling of deliverance communicated
by art as a token of another world, though to a psychologist this exaltation of art might be just Proust's way of
saying how much it exalted him. He felt that the imaginative, metaphorical character of art was essential to
it because only by breaking from everyday appearance
could art adumbrate the transcendent truth which he

believed to be its burden. For him art had a supernatural
sanction as categorical as Kant's imperative, though it
commanded artistic activity rather than obedience to an
abstract moral law.

Proust's attitude was Platonic and mystical and cannot
be shared by anyone who regards art as a natural part of
natural existence, a phenomenon subject to physiologi-
cal, psychological and sociological explanation like other
human activities. But his assertion of a divine promise
and summons in art may be taken as a poetic expression
of the value of art. Feeling it to be vastly more important than anything else, he seized upon the traditional
means of communicating supreme emotion. Following
the poets who have followed Plato, he fell back upon
reminiscence of another world to explain the spell of art,
though his individualism led him to think of each artist
as having descended from a unique eternity of his own.
Regardless of how literally Proust believed it, or how
much he prized it, if personal survival retained great attraction for many of his readers, then by linking art with
immortality he could count on evoking sympathy for his
emotion toward art. But he seems too sincere deliberately to have used such a device merely for effect. And
at times he confessed misgivings about the mystical interpretation. In the final volumes (though they apparently
are not the last he worked on) he did not count on personal immortality but faced death as the destruction of
the individual, whose work might survive fifty years before it also would disappear.

Despite his idea that art was something more than life,
he sometimes played with the notion that life could be
refined and stylized to the pitch of art. For him art was
music, painting, architecture, sculpture, theater, litera-

ture, and only through courtesy, humor or metaphor did
the other activities of man, which he lumped together as
" life," appear to him artistic, though in varying degrees
they might approach the value of art — including the
performance of the elevator boy who neatly avoided
halting his steel cage too soon or too late. When watching a head waiter carving duck as if he were going
through the motions of a great actor; when describing
as artistic the preparations for a party, the course of a
conversation or the conduct of a love affair; whenever
treating the skillful adaptation of means to ends as if it
constituted art, Proust was always conscious of the " as
if," expressed or implied, which was introduced by his
own imagination. For him the deft overcoming of difficulty alone was not art, but only suggestive of it, because
one of the elements in it. Equally short of art, though
analogous to it, were forms and rhythms observed in nature, or in a face, or in the involuntary aspects of behavior — all of which appealed to him as if appearing in
art — though here again it was the imaginative " as if "
added by the author that raised the experience to the
power of art. When he saw the artistic process where
no art would have been but for his own participation;
and when he saw an artistic result where no artist had
been at work but himself: he did not find art in life; he
superimposed art on life.

But in the end (at the end of the book if not of the
author's life) along with the disappearance of other distinctions that had seemed important, even the difference between life and art had to go, for he found them
coinciding as surely as he saw a *rapprochement* between the bourgeoisie and the aristocracy. When at
last he devoted himself to art with his whole being, he

felt a new affinity with Françoise who, if anyone, represented life in contrast to art. " I would work beside
her, and almost as she did (at least as she had formerly
done, for she was so old now that she could hardly see).
Pinning here and there a supplementary sheet, I would
construct a book, I dare not say ambitiously like a cathedral, but very simply like a dress. When I happened
not to have all my papers near me . . . and lacked just
the one I needed, Françoise well understood my annoy-
ance, she who had always said that she could not sew if
she did not have the number of thread and the buttons
that she needed, and because, as a result of living with
me, she had acquired a kind of instinctive understand-
ing of literary labor . . . [she] guessed my happiness
and respected my work. . . . As a result of pasting
them together . . . the papers got torn here and there.
When necessary, Françoise could help me strengthen
them in the same way that she patched the worn parts
of her dresses, or put a piece of newspaper in a broken
kitchen window, while waiting for the glazier as I waited
for the printer. . . . Pointing out my note-books,
chewed like wood that insects have got into, she would
say: ' It's all moth-eaten; look, it's too bad; here is the
edge of a page that is nothing but lace '; and, examining
it like a tailor, ' I'm afraid I can't mend it, it's done for.
It's a shame; it's probably your most beautiful thoughts.
As they say in Combray, no furrier knows as much as
the moths. They always get into the best material ' "
(Le Temps Retrouvé, II, 241, 242).

This tender reconciliation of art and life, however,
must be a triumph of art rather than a fact of life, or else
life is not so vain as Proust believed, and art is not so
vital as he insisted. If Françoise stood on the same level

as the artist, then life, as represented by her, was justified without the outside aid of art; and when art was
added, it did not add much to life as it was already being
lived. Françoise with her work was as self-sufficient as
Proust with his, and she was not unlike him in sensing
values in other lives. The existence of people like her
might redeem a world that even his art could not ran-
som. Yet we are indebted to his art for knowledge of
her life. Thanks to his writing we are grateful for her
existing. Through his romance we know that she was
real.

Few persons of culture were represented by Proust
as having half her discernment. In his novel only the
artists — Bergotte, Elstir, Vinteuil and the narrator —
were credited with real appreciation of art. Only fit-
fully could M. de Charlus or Swann, with all their refinement, rise to genuine aesthetic experience. The
" remarkable intellectual and artistic personality " of
Swann lifted him above others, but fell short of its fine
promise, because he never " produced " anything. He
would not even make the effort to appreciate art for
himself, but, when called upon to do so, would substitute information about a work for evaluation of it. Unable to become an artist himself, the best that Swann
could do with the stimulus of music was to assimilate it
to the pleasure of love. Music was wasted on him,
Proust felt, because, while it could constitute a summons, it could not create ability and make of Swann the
writer he never was (*Le Temps Retrouvé*, II, 23).

To Proust a mere aesthete was not only cut off from
life, but failed to appreciate art. He ridiculed and pitied
the " celibates of art " who " have the unhappiness of
the virginal and the lazy, and whom fecundity in work

would cure." Their artistic enjoyment is sterile because they do not make the effort to realize profound personal impressions. " But laughable as these amateurs are, they are not altogether to be disdained. They are nature's first attempts in trying to create the artist " (*Le Temps Retrouvé*, II, 43, 44).

Yet as he sometimes attributed artistic qualities to activities outside the sacred precincts of art, so he occasionally described aesthetes like the Baron and Swann as if they were artists. Fearing that he might have been unjust to Swann, Proust suggested that Swann, who in adolescence had fancied himself an artist, and who later dissipated his boyhood inspirations in frivolity, was after all an artist in the way he lived, and especially in the way he talked (*La Prisonnière*, I, 278). And Proust spoke of the Baron as " an artist expert in the matter of *fêtes*, who would withdraw his piece and refuse his assistance rather than condescend to concessions which he thought would compromise the result of the ensemble " (*La Prisonnière*, II, 38). Proust said, however, that M. de Charlus was never anything but an amateur in life, because when he made disturbing discoveries they were of no utility to him as they would have been to the imagination of a writer like Bergotte.

Remarking on the Baron's way of referring to society ladies as if they were actresses vying with each other in artistic talent, Proust said: " Since society is the realm of nothingness, there are between the merits of different ladies of society only insignificant degrees which can be madly magnified only by the rancour or the imagination of a M. de Charlus " (*La Prisonnière*, II, 100). This mixture of social and artistic categories was explained on the ground that the Baron's genuine eloquence was furnished only with trivial themes. But Proust's own genius was furnished largely with the same themes, and he used all his ingenuity to show that nothing is trivial when touched with the wand of art. Still, he hated to stretch art to include conversation, much as he admired good talk: " All who provide their intelligence with no other realization than conversation, that is, an imperfect realization, remain unsatiated even after hours together, and hang even more avidly on the exhausted interlocutor of whom they demand, in their error, a satisfaction which social pleasures are powerless to give " (*La Prisonnière*, II, 113).

Proust was right in declaring that he himself was not a pure aesthete, for he was not satisfied with art unless it had an ulterior meaning, nor was he content to appreciate without himself creating. Through long contemplation of the treasures stored in his private museum of recollection he had tried to become an aesthete like Swann, but could not rest until he was a writer like Bergotte. Proust said that mere aesthetic curiosity deserved the name of indifference compared to his tireless, tortured curiosity about Albertine. Contrasting his life with that of a collector, he asked: " What statues, what pictures long pursued, at last possessed, or even . . . contemplated with disinterestedness, could have given, . . . what can be known only by suffering it: the life of others? " (*La Prisonnière*, II, 251).

He realized that even if a person were an artist the fact might be slow in receiving recognition. He was well aware of the precariousness of his own ambition, especially after becoming convinced of the value of the work within him. Only by chance did Vinteuil's great *Septet* see the light of day — through a labor of love on

the part of his daughter's friend; and the first performance of it by Morel resulted from the weakness of the
Baron for his protégé rather than from devotion to
the music. It was easy for Mme. Verdurin to frighten
Morel into standing by her through threats of artistic
disaster if he should desert her to play at the houses of
her rivals, because he felt that it was not enough for
him to be an artist without having the right reputation.
But while real gifts needed patronage and luck to succeed, a person without talent might go far with backing
— like Rachel, whose recitation was saved from failure
when the Duchesse de Guermantes " decided the victory by crying, ' it is wonderful! ' right in the middle
of the poem which she thought perhaps had ended.
Several guests undertook then to underline this exclama-
tion with an approving look and an inclination of the
head to show, it may be, not so much their comprehen-
sion of the performer as their relations with the duchess "
(Le Temps Retrouvé, II, 195).

Elstir, the painter, appeared first in the " nucleus " of
the Verdurins, when his ability was attested only by the
faith they placed in any struggling artist loyal to them.
Upon his next appearance in the novel he was famous,
though not yet to the degree pretended by the proprie-
tor of the Rivebelle restaurant. One could fairly see
the artist's reputation in the making, through the questions tourists began to ask about how he lived; through
the number of letters he received from abroad; and
through the impression given by his remarkable industry. When the narrator became acquainted with him
he thought: " Could it be possible that this man of
genius, this sage, this recluse, this philosopher of mag-
nificent conversation who dominated everything, was

the ridiculous, perverse painter formerly adopted by the Verdurins? " (*Jeunes Filles*, III, 136). It seemed impossible to separate the value of an artist's work from the brilliancy of his career.

Finally Elstir became *à la mode*. Mme. de Guermantes displayed in her salon two of his drawings which she had formerly relegated to a cabinet upstairs. " Mme. de Guermantes could not console herself for having given so many of his paintings to her cousin, not because they were the fashion, but because she was enthusiastic about them now. Fashion, in fact, is constituted by the infatuation of a number of people of whom the Guermantes are representative. But she did not dream of buying other pictures of his, since for some time they had gone up to madly high prices. She wanted at least to have something by Elstir in her salon and had brought down these two drawings which she declared she ' preferred to his painting ' " (*Albertine Disparue*, II, 47, 48).

When M. Verdurin died the painter alone was grieved, because " as Elstir grew older he superstitiously tied his work to the society which had furnished him his models . . . and had given him his public. . . . It was for him a little of the beauty of his work which was eclipsed along with a little of what the universe had held in the way of awareness of this beauty " (*Le Temps Retrouvé*, I, 104, 105). Creating and being appreciated went together for the author, and if fame was not the goal of effort, it might be the only objective indication of success, even to the artist. Proust revealed how stimulating success was to him in confessing his feeling when an article of his was published and he read it over, trying to imagine the approval of invisible readers. There was a danger that the external evidence of achievement might be mistaken for the substance, but a similar risk was inevitable in any inference. Recognition followed the inner achievement at a considerable remove and might continue to follow blindly, as in the case of Bergotte who was still revered as a master when he died, though he had written nothing for twenty years.

It seemed to Proust, as to Croce, that the physical art object is merely a set of symbols for communicating the artist's intention to other people, and that the only way of gauging the quality of his performance is through its impression on them — if they are the right people. In the beginning only such as the Verdurins will take up an unrecognized artist. But, affected as their admiration may be, Proust showed that it cannot be less genuine than that of persons like the Guermantes who acclaim him later, while to the public a fine artist's reputation will seldom be more than a name.

At the final gathering with the Princesse de Guermantes, scarcely anyone recognized a supposedly familiar poem of La Fontaine recited by Rachel. And there was the young man who was exasperated when disturbed while listening to the Kreutzer Sonata which, " through being mistaken about the program, he believed to be a piece by Ravel that he had been told was as beautiful as something by Palestrina, though difficult to understand." The noise he made in changing his place caused several people to turn their heads, " for whom this simple exertion of looking around interrupted a little the torture of listening ' religiously ' to the Kreutzer Sonata " (*Le Temps Retrouvé*, II, 230).

But despite the shams of aestheticism the devious paths of Proust's thought always led back to the supreme im-

portance of art and the artist. He could not think of
one apart from the other, and it was inconceivable to
him that a genuine response to art should not involve
the wish to be an artist. Being an artist was to him the
end of art, as art was the fulfillment of life.

He deprecated the mere aesthete, yet seems to have
regarded artistic creation as the means of reaching the
deepest appreciation. His joy in the aesthetic attitude,
induced chiefly by art and inspiring him to be an artist,
lay in the release that Schopenhauer called relief from
the Will. For both men salvation lay in shifting from
the role of participant to that of appreciative onlooker;
and both found this transference facilitated not only by
the enjoyment of art but through reminiscence, which
Proust practically identified with his own art.

Schopenhauer said before Proust (or his teacher,
Bergson): "The remembrance of past and distant
scenes flits across our minds like a lost paradise." And:
"We imagine that the objective stood before us then
just as pure and undisturbed by any relation to the will
as its image stands in our fancy now; while in reality the
relation of the objects to our will gave us pain then just
as it does now. We can deliver ourselves from all suffering just as well through present objects as through
distant ones whenever we raise ourselves to a purely objective contemplation of them and so are able to bring
about the illusion that only the objects are present and
not we ourselves. . . . The world as idea alone remains and the world as will has disappeared."

Schopenhauer differed from Proust in attributing the
bliss of contemplation to the suppression of self. In the
Proustian version of the contemplative attitude, its mystical culmination is not the quietus but the apotheosis of

self with all its private, personal values. His art was devoted to preventing the transcendence of personality.

It is not contradictory that the " eternal man " in him, rising above pain and vanity, should incite the man of letters and be aided by him. Through writing Proust clung most tenaciously to the eternal essences which alone mattered in the flux of things. He did not prostitute his unworldly vision to worldly ambition. He was ambitious, but only to write; and he wrote to save his soul. He wanted to write supremely well, and rejoiced in every indication that he was becoming a great writer, because for him nothing else was worth doing, and because when he wrote well everything he was aware of had value, everything was redeemed.

It would have been a contradiction if he had devoted himself to art for the purpose of figuring more effectively as a man among men in the everyday world, because he regarded solitude as the first condition of artistic achievement. To some degree writing might indirectly bring him close to friends, but he realized that his work would soon supplant the need of their company; and, compared with the importance of art, he regarded social pleasures as the realm of nothingness. " The artist who renounces an hour of work for an hour of conversation with a friend knows that he sacrifices a reality for something that does not exist " (*Le Temps Retrouvé*, II, 20; cf. also, *ibid.*, pp. 176, 177). Elstir also had thought that through the fruits of his solitude he could reach people at a distance and be with them in spirit; but his work brought indifference to society, and the habit of isolation the love of it.

Proust's life would have been a failure if it had not led to writing. Any other goal than literature would have been a substitute. At first he may have wished to write partly in order to establish his worth retroactively among the people who held the stage in his youth — to cut a figure that would impress those who had dazzled him. He may have hoped that in becoming an artist he might become more of a person. But in the last analysis the only kind of person he cared to be was an artist. His art propped up his life in so far as he used writing to edit his existence and make it readable where it had been scarcely bearable; but on the final level of motivation he exploited his life as mere stuff and stimulus for art.

One cannot seriously entertain an ideal without hoping and striving to attain it, and Proust was imbued with the romantic ideal of artistic genius. He admired artists because he felt (even before thinking it out) that art was the bridge from time to eternity. So it fascinated him to trace the inner development of the artist in himself and in Elstir, and Proust's novel reveals what it feels like to be an artist, what his inner processes are, his motives and moods. The substance of the revelation is that "the data provided by life do not count for the artist except as opportunities for him to unsheathe his genius"; and that the so-called beauty of life is a stage this side of art (where Swann stopped) to which the creative artist falls back when his power is spent (Cf. *Jeunes Filles*, III, 120, 121).

Proust ranked artists, and particularly great writers, so far above the rest of mankind that he was shocked to think that writing might not be anything remarkable after all, that to write " is for the writer a healthy and necessary function the accomplishment of which makes him happy, as for athletic men to exercise, sweat and bathe " (*Le Temps Retrouvé*, II, 57). He was such a hero-worshiper that he was eager to meet Elstir before seeing any of his paintings, and was immediately so impressed that he said Elstir's friendliness " was as superior to that of Saint-Loup as his to the affability of a *petit bourgeois*. Beside that of a great artist the friendliness of a *grand seigneur*, charming as it may be, has the air of play-acting, of simulation. Saint-Loup sought to please; Elstir loved to give, to give himself . . ." (*Jeunes Filles*, III, 88). Swann, to whom Proust attributed the turning points of his life, and whose taste he sought to acquire, was a delicate needle pointing to the genius of men like Elstir and Vinteuil and, trusting in Swann, Proust steered by compass, as it were, toward art beyond his horizon.

When Octave, a young man who seemed to have no serious interests, turned out to be an artist of a high order, Proust explained that art must have been something so intimate for him, dwelling so far down in the secret folds of his being, that it never occurred to him to mention it. With the consciousness of having nearly completed a masterpiece, Proust added: " Who knows but what, seen externally, a certain man of talent, or even a man without talent, but loving things of the mind — myself for example — might have given . . . the impression of the most consummate and pretentious ass " (*Albertine Disparue*, II, 83).

Through art Proust not only saved himself, but has gone far toward saving his admirers by endowing them with the gift of his perceptions, his way of seeing and feeling. He was justified in saying that his readers are really their own readers, his book a magnifying glass with which they may read themselves (Cf. *Le Temps*

Retrouvé, II, 240). Into his art he brought all that he had loved, sharing it with them, and they find in him the essence of their lives, so unmistakably their own that they love him as themselves, so well expressed that they rely on him to give the meaning of their most intimate experience. Had Proust not lived to write, his readers might as well not have lived at all, unless they could have become their own Proust, or have found someone else to kindle for them, in the midst of life, the transfiguring fire of art.

I I

George Santayana

GEORGE SANTAYANA

References to George Santayana in contemporary thought drift through a reader's consciousness like the breath of a strange flower. In the first intimations of his existence there is nothing to suggest a name to conjure with, except the name itself. In the course of a book on metaphysics or an article on epistemology he will be mentioned as having made a point with which the writer agrees or disagrees, yet one scarcely feels that here is merely another professor whose importance consists in contributions to the footnotes of his fellows. It is surprising that he writes in English, and one wonders where the soft syllables of his name might be native. But whatever may be imagined about him, the truth is remarkable enough.

He himself has said: " How came a child born in Spain of Spanish parents to live in Boston and write the English language? " The answer to this question is, of course, a matter of biography, and biography may also explain why the boy became philosophical, though nothing but his being himself can explain the quality of his mind. He was practically an only child, being the only one of his mother's second marriage. When he was lonely and wondered what to do he would say to his parents, "Entertain me! " But his mother was cold to him, because she had lost her first son very early and felt that her other children were inferior beings. So the young Santayana looked on with detachment at home as well as in Boston and the world. When he came to write on the family, he said: " It takes patience to appreciate domestic bliss; volatile spirits prefer unhappiness. Young men escape as soon as they can, at least in fancy, into the wide world; all prophets are homeless and all inspired artists; philosophers think out some communism or other, and monks put it in practice " (*The Life of Reason*, II, 45).

From the beginning he was obliged to find in imagination the remedy for loneliness. His connection with his family as persons was adventitious and temporary, perhaps less important than his associations at Harvard, though they also were merely part of the environment in which he found himself before he was able to resign and live in Europe with the past that nourished his true self. His loyalty has always been to what he loved rather than to what he happened to live with. To him no ties are morally binding but those of common thoughts and purposes. Instead of allowing the accident of family, country or profession to dictate his affection and his future, he has followed his affinities and aspirations. Even the age he chanced to live in has not kept him from communing with the ancients he admires.

When he began to teach philosophy at Harvard he was twenty-six, only a few years older than many of his students. He had something of the English idea of professor and students living together and during his first years of teaching he lived with undergraduates. This lasted until he was about thirty-five and then died of itself. He enjoyed teaching when he was in the mood for it, because he liked young people and liked talking with them, as he enjoyed a dinner or any social pleasure. It is said that to hear him lecture was like listening to Brahms; and that at the end of his last class the students applauded for twenty minutes while he stood, not knowing what to do.

The students even got him interested in football, so much so that he went to practice as well as to every game. "It was partly the romance of the thing that attracted me," he said; "but partly the influence of the boys. It was easy to catch fire." To be interested in athletics as an undergraduate is not unusual, but his was a belated interest. It may have been partly a result of growing admiration for the Greeks and realization of the important place held in their culture by Olympia. The "Athletic Ode," included among his *Poems*, bears this out; and in *The Life of Reason* he said of character training: "Priceless in this regard is athletic exercise; for here the test of ability is visible, the comparison is not odious, the need of co-operation is clear, and the consciousness of power genuine and therefore ennobling. Socratic dialectic is not a better means of learning to know oneself " (II, 49).

He did not live a very professorial life at Harvard — being thrown with undergraduates in Cambridge and going out to parties in Boston; not to dances, for he did not dance, but to dinners. Once he went to three in the same week and sat next to the same lady each time — in the same dress! He chuckled in telling of her chagrin. " She never thought the same people would be invited. I can see the dress to this day: blue, and trimmed with artificial pearls. . . . At these dinners you talked half an hour with the lady on one side, then half an hour with the lady on the other side, then the first one

again; about ten minutes with the men alone; and finally, in the drawing room, you were able to choose the
lady you wished to talk to. I didn't like the men much.
Even Roger Wolcott, the former governor of Massa-
chusetts, was uninteresting. He came from a good family, had wealth, and was successful in politics — everything to make him important. I had looked forward to
meeting him, but I was very much disappointed. He
had enough mind to have opinions, but not enough to
have the right ones. But I liked the ladies of Boston
and enjoyed talking with them. They had traveled,
read, and were cultivated — much more so than the
men."

As for the philosophy department then: " The com-
bination was interesting, but we were all commonplace.
When Muensterberg came he was commonplace too,
but he brought something different, a new element.
Then there was Palmer; he is still vegetating there.
William James was a moody person. Well, perhaps
not moody, because he wasn't gloomy. One day he'd
say to Mrs. James: ' How serene Palmer is; what a calm,
wise, active person! ' The next day he'd exclaim to
her: ' What a hypocrite Palmer is, what an intriguing
old woman! ' Mrs. James was a very steadying influence on him; she led him along slowly but surely.
James had money. That is, he had something beyond
his professor's salary — four thousand dollars was the
usual sum in those days — so that he could have a comfortable home. Poor Royce didn't have a thing except
his salary, and the contrast between the way he lived
and the way James did was very marked. They both
had children and Royce's four thousand dollars was
simply not enough, though it went further than it would

today. I was younger than most of the men, of course, and didn't count for much. I think I count for more now."

While Mr. Santayana likes to recall the past he does not seem wistful about it, because he is happy in a life filled as nearly as possible with his real interests, and to the same degree emptied of distractions. He lives in Rome, without family, colleagues or countrymen, but often sees his old friend, the philosopher and psychologist, C. A. Strong, with whom he has lived from time to time. He values friends, though many of them are dead, including those he used to visit in English country houses. Friends are always close to him in imagination, and he enjoys seeing them when they come to Rome, though he remarked with a chuckle: "I am like the Pope — I don't return visits."

He would prefer a world more favorable to friendship, and has said that for it to flourish "personal life would have to become more public and social life more simple and humane. . . . The ancients, so long as they were free, spent their whole life in forum and palaestra, camp, theater, and temple, and in consequence could live by friendship even in their maturer years" (*The Life of Reason*, II, 156). Since the indispensable thing in friendship is common interests, and an important factor is living together, "The tie that in contemporary society most nearly resembles the ancient ideal of friendship is a well-assorted marriage" (*ibid.*, II, 156). His *Sonnets* may explain why this was not for him, if the sufficient explanation is not that as a man apart he was destined to live alone.

Instead of telephoning him his friends are likely to write him a note which he can answer at leisure, since

he has said that the telephone is a convenience when a
person wants to be at a distance in an instant, but not
when he is where he wants to be and doing what he
wishes. Lunch is his most convenient time for seeing
friends, and he likes to get away from the hotel after a
morning of writing, unless a hard rain keeps him in his
room all day, " and that's very pokey." He prefers to
eat where Italians do, as his hotel is full of English-
speaking people; and between lunch and tea he takes a
walk.

He says that walking is the best exercise for a philosopher, and usually strolls alone, unaware of traffic
except when the difficulty of talking makes him realize
the noise. In the middle of the street, with cars whizzing
all around him, he said by way of reassurance, " They
don't run over you." He likes to climb the Spanish
Steps for a turn on the Pincio where he enjoys the view
over the Piazza del Popolo, with the dome of St. Peter's
in the distance. He takes pleasure in the shade of the
trees but does not know their names, because he is city-
bred. To him the charm of the Borghese Gardens is
their verdure. Here and there they suggest to him a
passage in Virgil or Horace, and the stadium by the tall
umbrella pines reminds him of a Greek tragedy he heard
in Athens. He has a bench in the sun where he sits on
cool days, and a shady one, against the rocks near the
temple of Esculapius, that he saves for warm weather.
As he likes to read in the open, he often cuts apart an
unbound book and carries a section of it in his pocket —
enough for one sitting.

The Forum is one of his haunts, but he does not learn
the names of the ruins because he would only forget
them. Looking down from the Palatine, however, he

recognized at least one temple, for he remarked: " The Caesars had a good view of the Vestal Virgins." He seldom goes to museums and churches any more, " because they make me tired in the small of my back, and it takes too much self-control to look at only one or two things." Having seen all the show-places he has no curiosity about what is there, but he does like to go to the Pantheon, which is more religious to him than most churches. He also goes to San Pietro in Vincoli, " for the *Moses* of Michelangelo, which is one of the things I like." He used to walk out to San Paolo Fuori le Mura, but now he lets that wait until Strong comes with his car.

Mr. Santayana likes to be inconspicuous. Traveling in the East he let his beard grow to save himself trouble, and when he came back to Harvard everyone exclaimed, " Why, you have a beard! " So he kept it (four years in all) to avoid having people say, " Oh, but you've shaved off your beard! " He said: " A man doesn't like that all the time, and so I waited until I reached New York, and the day I sailed for Europe I had it removed." He used to smoke, " though I never liked the taste of tobacco in my mouth. I smoked because others did and we are creatures of habit and occasion. It gave me the sense of doing something in common — but anything will give it. Walking will do it; a stick will do it. I always carry a stick, though I was hooted for it in Chicago." He dresses all in black, doubtless in order to pass unnoticed, and it may be for the same reason, as well as for convenience, that he prefers not to carry a book in his hand. When a head waiter makes a fuss over him, repeating how glad he is to see *il Signore* looking so well — " *Il Signore* never changes, for years he has looked the same " — he seems to wish he might check his body and personality.

Like his dark, well-fitting clothes, his speech attracts no attention and gives no clue to his origin, for only modesty could have prompted him to say in his autobiographical sketch that he learned to speak English " without a marked accent." At least to non-philological ears he speaks it without any accent — Spanish, American or British. He enjoys using his native tongue but seldom has the opportunity. Whether he is addressed in English or Italian he replies gently in the same language, though he says he uses Italian " only for the frictions of life " and prefers English or French for discussion. " But the French speak so rapidly that, well as I know French, at the theater in Paris it takes me fifteen minutes to understand what is being said." He had two years of study in Germany and remarked that German is much easier to understand than French or Italian because it cannot be pronounced fast.

" Some day I shall write on the American drawl. I have a theory that it is caused by pragmatism. The pragmatists know what to do, and talking about it is a mere concession, like talking to a child; so they drawl or joke."

He grew up knowing Latin naturally, from his love of reading it. As an undergraduate at Harvard he took a course in Latin composition, did not go to the class but wrote all the exercises and got ninety in the course. The translation of Spinoza's *Ethics* for which he wrote a preface greatly disappointed him, " because there were many errors. It was done by someone who had only the Latin he had learned in school." He said he had learned to write English from reading French, and deprecated Barrett Wendell's now popular idea of teaching English as such, because men used to write it better when they studied other languages instead.

Mr. Santayana is familiar with many countries as well as their languages, for, with his aloofness, he has always been a man of the world. He loves Spain. " She has a personality of her own, though her ancient ruins aren't so grand as those of Italy; her Gothic is a Spanish Gothic, and she might look shabby after Italy. I had a place in the backwoods of Spain where I loved to be among the common people. It wasn't really backwoods," he laughed, " because there wasn't a tree in sight."

He thinks it is more interesting for an American to visit the Continent than England. " England isn't different enough; where it is different, it is unpleasantly so to him. England is only half way — he isn't at home and he isn't away — but in Italy he gets his range. There are castles and cathedrals in England, but she has put her best into books and boats, and afternoon tea in the garden."

At times he seems partially to identify himself with the English, and is like an English gentleman in dignity and regard for decorum. He always reads *The Morning Post* after breakfast, " because I am something of an old fogey." He said, however, that he could not appreciate *Alice in Wonderland* as the English do, and thought it might be because he was not Anglo-Saxon. Great as his affection for the English is, when he soliloquized about England, as when he wrote *Character and Opinion in the United States,* he did so with the objectivity of one making a visit from afar. He is a cosmopolite detached from all countries: from his native Spain, from the United States he grew up in, from England where he sojourned

in maturity, and from Italy where he lives now, looking on.

He picks out the Spanish theological students from
the others by the blue on their gowns. He notices frag-
ments uncovered in the new excavations. He is pleased
to find a baroque doorway between two worthless buildings, " a thing that would be one of the sights if it were
anywhere else." From his window he watches the pa-
rades on the twenty-first of April, the birthday of Rome.
" Even small boys wear the black shirt of the Fascists,
with a blue neckerchief, grey shorts, and a black fez with
a tassel. There's nothing to it, but it catches." He sees
the Pope carried on his red velvet sedia, " escorted like
Cleopatra by two great fans of peacock feathers." There
is always something in the Eternal City that he might
have had in mind when he wrote in *The Sense of Beauty:*
" What is in itself a gorgeous and unmeaning ornament,
by its absolute impressiveness becomes a vivid symbol
of those other ultimates which have a similar power over
the soul " (p. 75).

He usually leaves Rome in June to escape the heat, and
goes to Cortina in what was the Austrian Tyrol, or to
Switzerland, or to Paris; and if Paris gets hot — " to some
watering place." But he regards Rome as his base from
now on: " If I'm alive you'll find me here." He lives in
Rome because there he feels closer to the past than anywhere else. He thinks that Greece has changed too
much, now that the Greeks have become Orientalized,
whereas Rome has never lost her grandeur — " and
Rome is a more civilized place to live in than Athens."

The greatness of Rome is most evident in architecture,
the art which he understands best; and it was architecture with all its associations that he most enjoyed on his

travels. He was especially impressed by the ruins at
Baalbek, which he thought grander than anything in
Rome. He recalled the domes and minarets of Constan-
tinople as seen from the ship entering the harbor, and
felt that Santa Sophia was the sort of thing that would
grow on him. Remembering his months in Egypt and
weeks on the Nile, he mentioned that he did not feel
at all secure on the donkey trips, as he was not used to
riding. " There was a ring on my saddle in front, just
big enough to hook my little finger through, and I suppose it didn't really help me to stay on but it made me
feel safer." He did not visit the Valley of the Kings
because no architecture was there and he wanted to see
again the immense temples of Karnak, the pylons, colon-
nades and obelisks in the sun. " I had been to Karnak
in the morning with an excursion, but that afternoon I
went alone and had a beautiful time."

The Parthenon he thought would be better now than
when he saw it — " with more of the columns stood up."
In looking at the Erectheum he saw what is meant by the
saying that the Ionic style is feminine. " The four tall
Ionic columns and the doorway of the north porch I
think the most beautiful architecture anywhere." He
loves form in itself, but has written: " The profit of
travel, and the extraordinary charm of all visible relics
of antiquity, consists in the acquisition of images in
which to focus a mass of discursive knowledge not otherwise felt together " (*The Sense of Beauty*, p. 211).

" The sky is over all countries," he once wrote; and
though his late birth banished him from ancient Athens
where he would have been most at home, he does not
complain of exile, and he is not apprehensive. " For
myself, even if I could live to see it, I should not be afraid

of the future domination, whatever it may be. One has
to live in some age, under some fashion; I have found, in
different times and places, the liberal, the Catholic, and
the German air quite possible to breathe; nor, I am sure,
would communism be without its advantages to a free
mind, and its splendid emotions " (*Soliloquies in England*, p. 188).

He restricts himself to what is important for him,
though he lives in a modern hotel like Proust rather than
in a garret like Spinoza, and always travels first class.
He said: " I asked my father why he traveled third class
and he answered, ' Because there's no fourth.' " He
does not want a house lest he become a prey to collecting
antiques; the problem of looking after it and managing
servants also occurs to him. Somewhere he has written
that wealth and possessions enslave a man, and has expressed a preference for public conveyances and waiters.
His individualism is not the kind that dreads collectivism.

In 1932 he had been without his library for some time,
having left most of his books in Strong's villa at Fiesole.
" That is better than not having them at all, because now
and then I can send for one. Lately I sent for my
Spinoza and was glad to have it back." His room had
scarcely any space for books and he was looking forward
to a larger sitting room next year, with more of his books.
He was pleased with a new Shakespeare he had ordered
from a catalogue, " though to my surprise the volumes
were many and large." He smiled: " Now that I have
such a good foundation for a library I certainly must
have a new bookcase." In his room is a trunk containing
relics from his Harvard days, and an immense gold medal
given him by the British Royal Society of Literature
for the excellence of his prose.

He has simplified living in order to enrich life. " To substitute the society of ideas for that of things is simply to live in the mind; it is to survey the world of existences in its truth and beauty rather than in its personal perspectives, or with practical urgency. It is the sole path to happiness for the intellectual man, because the intellectual man cannot be satisfied with a world of perpetual change, defeat and imperfection. It is the path trodden by ancient philosophers and modern saints or poets; not, of course, by modern writers on philosophy (except Spinoza), because these have not been philosophers in the vital sense; they have practiced no spiritual discipline, suffered no change of heart, but lived on exactly like other professors " (*Soliloquies in England*, p. 120).

He said one day: " A philosopher has to give up a good many things, but he shouldn't do it grudgingly. I wouldn't want to be a ranting philosopher like Carlyle or a sighing one like Matthew Arnold." To people who think of a materialist and naturalist as a loose person it is hard to understand his integrity and restraint, his almost other-worldly renunciation of much that might seem innocent. They fail to see how natural it is for him to find happiness in his way; how easy it is for him to be himself. If he is not doing all the things he might have enjoyed, he sees the impossibility of that and accepts it. Since he could not have all that human life affords he chose the best, according to his own taste and imagination, and let the rest go. He was fortunate in being able to do this; the opportunity does not come to everyone; but few have the intelligence to seize the chance, or the courage. Knowing that his way of life would not please everyone, he has written that happiness is " for each man after his own heart and for each hour according to its inspiration " (*Soliloquies in England*, p. 258). And: " The happy filling of a single hour is so much gained for the universe at large " (*The Life of Reason*, III, 270).

If a man follows the path that Mr. Santayana has chosen, " the world regards his way of living afterwards as rather ghostly and poor. But he usually congratulates himself upon it in the end; and of those who persevere some become saints and some poets and some philosophers " (*Soliloquies in England*, p. 121). " My detachment from things and persons is also affectionate, and simply what the ancients called philosophy: I consent that a flowing river should flow; I renounce that which betrays, and cling to that which satisfies " (*ibid.*, p. 247). " It is because I love life that I wish to keep it sweet so as to love it altogether " (*ibid.*, p. 258).

He finds his happiness in retirement because he believes that " natural society long ago proved a moral failure. It could not harmonize nor decently satisfy the instincts on which it rests. Hence the philosophers have felt bound not only to build themselves a superstructure, but to quit the ground floor " (*ibid.*, p. 121). If one has instincts and interests that cannot be satisfied in society, either they must be starved and allowed to atrophy, or one must seek a way of life in which they can flourish.

Only as a child did Mr. Santayana ask to be entertained. One cannot imagine him bored or turning to detective stories for relaxation. Intellectual work is not a strain on him. " It's no trouble for me to think, because I think only of what occurs to me. If I had a problem to solve, that would be terrible! " Feeling no pressure but his own interest he approaches the most serious subjects leisurely and with humor. " Since I have nothing to do, sometimes I think I don't get much done; it's so easy to waste time. . . . I felt an earthquake once at five in the morning but when I asked the lift man about it he said he hadn't felt it, ' because we who work sleep soundly! ' " Mr. Santayana chuckled: " As if I were an idler! " Referring in the same tone to Paul Shorey's dismissal of him as " that dainty, unassimilated man," he said: " If a piece of food can't be assimilated it must have some bone to it! "

In what for other people would be off-moments, Mr. Santayana does not slough off his mind like a hat, or deliberately limit his attention to things of no real interest, to prevent a nervous breakdown. He is always himself, with all his faculties intact, because his life is not artificially split into business and pleasure, work and play. He is not a professional man devoid of personality part of the time and a person without a calling the rest of the time. He is not like Hume who dismissed his philosophy when he came out of the study to join his friends. Mr. Santayana would not have a philosophy that he could not live by, and his philosophy is first of all a way of life, a full-bodied wisdom that is more than words.

He not only lives as he wishes but thinks his own thoughts and expresses them independently, as a man can who has nothing to gain by currying favor and nothing to fear from disapproval. Believing that reason is at bottom irrational, that one can make no distinctions between good and bad or have any genuine notion of excellence without a strong personal bias, he is dogmatic on principle. For every idea suggested to him he is ready with an answer thought out or with a fresh response radiating from the axis of his being. He entertains influences from every quarter; there is nothing he will not consider; but he never abandons his base. He said (in a letter): " I feel that there is a center, having some moral consistency and continuity, beneath the surface of experience, a center from which and by which particulars are distinguished: and in consequence my whole philosophy has an order or hierarchy in it, which an empiricist does not recognize."

The man and the author are one; which explains the vitality of his writing and the charm of his conversation. His vigorous neck and shoulders are behind the impact of his sentences, and the direct gaze of reddish brown eyes unusually clear and wide. A firm mouth and perfect teeth are in the solidity of his style. The urbanity of his manner is in his pages; the smoothness of his white skin; the frequent laugh and the hermetic smile. The fine head is bald in front, the hair above the ears and around the back is white; the moustache below the long nose is iron-grey; but seventy years and renunciation have renewed his joyful wisdom. He seems to understand everything; he loves some things; and fears nothing. He knows himself like Socrates, and looks on with the equilibrium of a god. " The time will doubtless come for each of us, if not for the universe at large, to cease from care; but our passage through life will have added a marvellous episode to the tale of things; and our distinction and glory, as well as our sorrow, will have lain in being something in particular, and in knowing what it is " (*The Realm of Essence*, p. xiv).

To be in Rome, talking with a sage who compares with the ancients, causes one to feel like a wanderer from the present scene talking in Limbo with the shade of Democritus, who has for ages been aware of what was happening on earth, who has even visited an American university, and who has read the latest books when they interested him. There is nothing shadowy about Mr. Santayana, but he has the detachment of Democritus, and the laughter. He said (in a letter): "You may find in my *Soliloquies in England* that I regard all existence as comic; whereas essence may be lyrical and truth tragic. And if a man goes about laughing at himself and at all the world, that does not exclude, but rather implies, that in other directions he discerns standards or points of reference which make this world seem ridiculous."

His view of life as primarily harmony, and of reason and art as rounding out life, is put to the test by tragedy. He confessed: "I didn't discuss tragedy as much as I should have in *The Sense of Beauty*. What I said was weak and I'd like to put in an appendix correcting that. I said that tragedy pleases, not on account of the pain in it, but on account of the elements that outweigh the pain. Now I think people like a certain amount of fright and suffering, within limits of course, although I think people might be refined beyond the enjoyment of tragedy. I am not a particularly sensitive person but there are some passages in *Lear* that I can't stand. And the play of *Tosca*, done by Sarah Bernhardt, where the girl hears the cries of her tortured lover and knows that he can be relieved only if she betrays him, which she has sworn not to do — I wasn't near to fainting but I had to get up and walk out. It is terrible." Neither could he read Proust's account of the lingering death of his grandmother.

It is doubtful whether Mr. Santayana's books would have the same charm if he had not suffered and striven to avoid pain, though he would not give this as the reason why he came to hold with Proust that there are "pure and positive values in life." He will not, like Proust,

" embrace the paradox that without evil no good whatever is conceivable." Mr. Santayana does not believe that the elimination of pain would mean the cessation of life or the value of it. " The senses would still be open, the instincts would still operate, and lead all creatures to the haunts and occupations that befitted them. The variety of nature and the infinity of art, with the companionship of our fellows, would fill the leisure of that ideal existence. These are the elements of our positive happiness, the things which, amid a thousand vexations and vanities, make the clear profit of living " (*The Sense of Beauty*, pp. 30, 31).

But while he has been fortunate in escaping the ills of Proust he is none the less aware of evil surrounding happiness:

> As in the crevices of Caesar's tomb
> The sweet herbs flourish on a little earth:
> So in this great disaster of our birth
> We can be happy and forget our doom.
> For morning, with a ray of tenderest joy
> Gilding the iron heaven, hides the truth,
> And evening gently woos us to employ
> Our grief in idle catches. Such is youth;
> Till from that summer's trance we wake, to find
> Despair before us, vanity behind.
>
> (From *Sonnet* XXV)

In the prologue to *Soliloquies in England* are " desperate verses " wrung from him by the war, and he says: " The artist playing a farce for others suffers a tragedy in himself. When he aspires to shed as much as possible the delusions of earthly passion, and to look at things joyfully and unselfishly, with the clear eyes of youth, it it not because he feels no weight of affliction, but precisely because he feels its weight to the full, and how final it is " (p. 6).

Perhaps this awareness of evil is most evident in his retreat to the realm of essence, which contains the form of all that exists, all that is to come, what has gone before, and things that never will exist. Not only the ideas which have been thought but those that never will occur to anyone, the plots of unwritten novels, the poems of inglorious Miltons — are essences. Whether they happen to be manifested in existence or not, they subsist timelessly for contemplation, like a vast dictionary of all conceivable and inconceivable words. Essences do not pass, and no one can deny them. In holding fast to them one is beyond becoming, doubting or dying. Man, like the rest of nature, tramps along a narrow road to victory and defeat; but, as mind, he can rise above the ranks to look down upon himself and the whole army of existence from the heights of complete detachment. Thence the oncoming generations are waves breaking on the beach of eternity, while the sun of truth shines on the everlasting realm of essence.

Yet it may be unfair to call this interest in essence a retreat, because while essences transcend life they also pervade it and are in a sense the only realities in it. They are the forms, qualities, or natures of all things, without which nothing could be what it is. For Mr. Santayana the aesthetic aspect of an object — its form — is its metaphysical essence; and every object is aesthetic when it becomes a focus for the pleasure of contemplation.

His form or essence seems to be self-contained, yet Mr. Santayana approaches Proust in appreciation of its " ideal relations " or associations. The difference is that Proust thinks of associations as an amplification of form, and accordingly is not disturbed when they distract him from a pattern actually before him; while Mr. Santayana is apprehensive lest they lead him into vague incoherence. He is classical enough to protest when the subjective or romantic factor predominates over what is objectively given. He values imagination but does not want it to blur the achievement of life or art and so degenerate into sentimentalism.

At the same time his classicism is romantic in that his readiness to recognize what is given enables him, like Proust, to see the unacademic beauties of each new environment. He also admits the subjective bias behind discrimination. And when he points out the danger of indeterminateness in *The Sense of Beauty* all he insists upon is that "whenever beauty is really seen and loved, it has a definite embodiment: the eye has precision, the work has style, and the object has perfection."

On the other hand, the romanticism of Proust is classic, because he was never satisfied with his memories until he had given them the sharpness of original impressions and the structure of ultimate art. Nor did he achieve this through make-believe, but through arduous attention to qualities which seemed to him objective and to have a claim upon him. Hence he has something of the "great variety" and certainly the "precision of characterization" that Mr. Santayana has admired in Shakespeare. If *The Sense of Beauty* argues that "progress lies in the direction of discrimination and precision, not in that of formless emotion and reverie," *The Remembrance of Things Past* has proved that emotion and reverie, when they are discriminated, become inexhaustible sources of form.

In *The Sense of Beauty* " expression is the quality acquired by objects through association." Proust would agree with this, but his work shows this to be no less the definition of form than of expression. Mr. Santayana is not ready, like Croce, to accept the identification of form and expression implicit in Proust, but does admit that expression (association) " can give images the same hold upon our attention which might be secured by a fortunate form or splendid material."

This is one reason why Mr. Santayana took the time to read nearly all of Proust's novel, and liked it. " You might think some of his analyses tedious, but when you have had the very same perceptions yourself you are fascinated with the minuteness of his account." He added: " I was interested to find toward the last that he also had the idea of essences. It is impossible that he should have got it from me, but he had hit on the same thing."

If it was the same thing, then Mr. Santayana indirectly, at least, admitted relations in essences, for relations are the quintessence of essence for Proust. Yet Proust thinks of essences as somehow rising above the relativity and change in which they are discovered — as shadowing forth an eternal reality behind all process. How such a reality is related to the events of earthly existence is not clear in either of these men, but neither has any philosopher from Plato to Whitehead been able to solve this problem without appeal to mystical insight.

Mr. Santayana, moreover, must have seen fully demonstrated in Proust his own teaching that expression can be delightful despite the painfulness of the thing expressed. He has written that " we must find enough expression of good to make us endure the expression of evil," adding that the expression of truth is especially redeeming. For Proust the truth is the constant good in every expression, in every imaginative reaching out from the evanescent present to an overarching order. Proust would agree with *The Sense of Beauty* that " the desire for truth makes us welcome eagerly whatever comes in its name," even the truth about Albertine.

He corroborates what Mr. Santayana has written concerning glimpses of perfection which art strives to renew, though for Proust this perfection is not a liberation from self so much as a realization of the true self. Proust, who puts the aesthetic imperative uppermost, would question the authority given to morals over aesthetics in *The Sense of Beauty*, though the subserviency of beauty is interpreted in that book as not without its reward: " There is no situation so terrible that it may not be relieved by the momentary pause of the mind to contemplate it aesthetically." And for both men beauty is " a ground of faith in the supremacy of the good."

Both escape from action to aesthetic contemplation, yet both are tremendously interested in life and resolved to come to terms with it, though realizing how intractable it is. Mr. Santayana's plea for a rational poetry, a literature directly interested in the truth, showing the wonder and tragedy of existence, is met by Proust, whose motto might be a passage from *The Life of Reason:* " Scope is a better thing than suggestion, and more truly poetical. It has expressed what suggestion pointed to and felt in the bulk: it possesses what was yearned for " (IV, 114). And Mr. Santayana might have had Proust in mind when he said that the poet " needs genius to see things as they are and to dare to describe them ingenuously," letting idealization enter through selecting " what is pertinent to ultimate interests and can speak eloquently to the soul," though Proust uses elaboration as well as selection and does not confine himself to " ultimate interests."

Mr. Santayana might have been writing of Proust as well as of Homer (or himself) when he said: " A real thing, when all its pertinent natural associates are discerned, touches wonder, pathos and beauty on every side; the rational poet is one who, without feigning anything unreal, perceives these momentous ties, and presents his subject loaded with its whole fate, missing no source of worth which is in it, no ideal influence which it may have " (*The Life of Reason*, IV, 114). It needs only to be added that for Proust the reality of a thing is its " momentous ties."

These have become so absorbing to Mr. Santayana that whereas the human foreground concerned him in his early books, in his later work his interest has shifted to the natural and metaphysical background. " I wrote my books backward. I should have written my last ones first and the first ones last. It was after my study at Cambridge, when I was under the influence of Plato and Aristotle who aroused my interest in social organization, in religion and politics, that I wrote *The Life of Reason*. But I should have dealt with cosmic things first, because they are not so difficult as human problems which I could handle better now that I have read more and had more experience. For example, the life of Napoleon — how complicated such a subject is! It is far harder to be certain about Napoleon than about stars and atoms. While much is thinkable about them, relatively little can be discovered compared to what is discoverable about Napoleon." (Or about one's most

intimate friend, Proust would say.)   "When I had dis-
cussed social and moral problems I went on to other
things, and now I have become more willing to halt at
essences. It is not the category or theory of essence that
interests me, but each essence exhibited in things or
ideas: the landscape of nature and history."

Mr. Santayana believes knowledge of human life to be
a kind of tact picked up as one goes along if one is acute,
and a reader of biography and history, which on the
whole he is reading more than philosophy. As for social
control, he thinks the professors of social science know
nothing about it but that it can be taught. "Aristotle
did his best to teach it to Alexander, and did very well,
everything considered. It's a hard matter to judge,
because Alexander died so young. If he had lived he
might have become great like Julius Caesar."

Along with Mr. Santayana's detachment from the
realm where force flourishes, and his devotion to es-
sences devoid of efficacy, there is the fact that he once
wished to become an officer in the Spanish army. He
has an unfinished book on politics with the title of
Dominations and Powers; he respects the powers that be,
and admires men of action in whom the will is strong.
"Our friend here has something in common with
Caesar: I am a great admirer of Julius Caesar and of
Mussolini also. My friend Strong and I quarrel about
Caesar *versus* Cicero, who is Strong's hero. I consider
Caesar greater than Napoleon, not because Caesar was a
greater general, but because he saw what was possible at
his time and carried it out, whereas Napoleon did not
understand his age so well and tried something impossible which necessarily failed."

In keeping with his admiration of dictators Mr. San-

tayana has written: " Liberalism has merely cleared a
field in which every soul and every corporate interest
may fight with every other for domination. Whoever
is victorious in this struggle will make an end of liberalism; and the new order, which will deem itself saved, will
have to defend itself in the following age against a new
crop of rebels " (*Soliloquies in England*, p. 188).
He does not think warfare is worse today than formerly. " If you read Homer you will see that war was
never nice. In ancient times a defeated city was utterly
destroyed, all the men killed, the women and children
sold into slavery." He is not a panegyrist of war, however. " It is war that wastes a nation's wealth, chokes
its industries, kills its flower, narrows its sympathies,
condemns it to be governed by adventurers, and leaves
the puny, deformed and unmanly to breed the next generation. . . . Instead of being descended from heroes,
modern nations are descended from slaves; and it is not
their bodies only that show it " (*The Life of Reason*, II,
82, 83). But he believes there are occasional advantages
in being conquered: " What the Orient owes to Greece,
the Occident to Rome, India to England, native America
to Spain, is a civilization incomparably better than that
which the conquered people could ever have provided
for themselves " (*The Life of Reason*, II, 75).
He is most doubtful whether war should be got rid of,
and is convinced that it is an inevitable aspect of human
life unless there can be " a conquest of all warring nations by some imperial people " like the Romans. " Ah,
my delicate friends . . . you have not seen the worst
yet. You suppose that this war has been a criminal
blunder and an exceptional horror. . . . You are mistaken. This war has given you your first glimpse of the

ancient, fundamental, normal state of the world, your first taste of reality " (*Soliloquies in England*, p. 103).

He finds comfort in determinism. " I am a determinist especially with regard to myself, but that does not do away with conscience. A determinist will still say to himself: ' I have been a fool, I have done a stupid thing.' He gets rid of a morbid conscience, however, and does not try to hurt himself still more after doing something he shouldn't. But it is characteristic of Puritans not to want to be Puritans. They are always trying to get over it. In my novel Mrs. Picklesworth (whose real name is Mrs. Anderson) says: ' Every night before I go to sleep I think over everything for fear I may have been too particular.' "

But while he believes in accepting the universe, including himself, he said: " Of course you can know what you prefer. For instance, a short time ago I was dizzy. I went to my doctor who found the cause of the trouble at once: I had been taking a certain medicine too consecutively. . . . I am pushing the point a little far," he chuckled; " it might be better for me to be dizzy than not. But I knew I very much preferred not to be! "

In his theory of the relation between mind and body he gives to the willing, active being the name of psyche; and along with it goes spirit, or awareness, which does not control or decide. Decisions are made in the psyche, and they result from the whole of experience, including heredity and environment. When decisions have happened to a person he can see what has occurred, but the feeling that he has a choice or that he has chosen comes in consciousness afterward. Mr. Santayana thinks this problem of the body-mind relation is independent of the question of the freedom of the will. " While I am a de-

terminist, it is not true of me in the strict scientific sense
of thinking that events can be *deduced logically* from
one another. I say that existence is contingent perva-
sively, but not monotonous."

Being a materialist he is always interested to see an
opponent admit his position, as Bergson does in granting
that life, which supposedly moves along of its own ac-
cord, is forced by circumstances into this or that channel.
" Those circumstances *are* material necessity." He had
just begun to read Bergson's book, *Les Deux Sources de
la Morale et de la Religion*, and remarked: " He is off on
his anthropology when he says the idea of immortality
grew up with people who longed for an after-life.
Primitive men sometimes dreamed of the dead or felt
them lingering about, and so imagined a fearful, shadowy
existence in another world. They believed in immortality not because they wanted to but because they
couldn't help it."

As for Mr. Dewey's idea that when a man is con-
fronted with a problematic situation he has a chance to
introduce a free choice, " That is a lingering supernaturalism." And Mr. Santayana might have quoted what
he had written of choice: " ' The die is cast,' said Caesar,
feeling a decision in himself of which he could neither
count nor weigh the multitudinous causes; and so says
every strong and clear intellect, every well-formed
character, seizing at the same moment with comprehensive instinct both its purposes and the means by which
they shall be attained. Only the fool, whose will signi-
fies nothing, boasts to have created it himself " (*The
Life of Reason*, I, 217).

" Dewey has two philosophies: empiricism and idealism, which he has never reconciled. His description of

thought is all very well and good except that it leaves thought out. I can understand James, but Dewey is different. He uses every word wrong. When the pragmatists talk about mind the way they do, they aren't dealing with what people ordinarily mean by mind. And to try to get at the inner experience of a mystic by a behavioristic approach never gets beyond the behavior of the mystic — it doesn't touch what is real to him. But Dewey seen behavioristically makes sense. I used to tell my students: ' If you read an author and he seems absurd, read him in such a way that he won't, because he didn't seem absurd to himself.' "

Mr. Santayana then observed that the germ of his own philosophy was in his poetry and that it had never changed. " I couldn't write poetry any more, because I feel restricted by its limitations and because I feel too little emotion. But prose can be as poetical as poetry. There is some poetry in my own writing. My book on *Matter* has some purple passages in it. People told me I ought not to put them in, but I wanted them there." He smiled, as if recalling the pleasure of composition when an idea " lights the fuse and precipitates the phrases."

In discussing his idea of religion as poetry he said: " That is like an advertisement — *Religion as Poetry*. If you take religion in the scholastic sense, and poetry in the scholastic sense, there isn't any connection. Still I think there is something in it. I got the idea from Matthew Arnold who had a great influence on me when I was young. Of course that's an old book now, but I don't take it back. I think that whatever truth religion has is poetic. And now they say the same of science! " He chuckled heartily.

"By religion I don't mean James's kind of religious experience, but rather the religion of the man who is religious without thinking about it. I have observed particularly the common people of Spain, for whom a certain way of acting is accepted toward God as another way of acting is accepted toward the ladies." And he laughed again. "When James was doing his book on *Varieties of Religious Experience* he asked me one day: 'Haven't you got some queer, out-of-the-way evidence to give me?' 'No,' I said; 'I read only orthodox authors like St. Teresa.' William James burst out: 'I won't have anything of her. She's always flirting with Christ!' And he added more which I can't repeat." Mr. Santayana enjoyed privately, but to the full, James's unmentionable words.

He identifies religion with some belief in the supernatural, though he mentioned that in his novel he has a professor of applied Christianity — "Christianity without the supernaturalism but with all the moral fervor. That is a legitimate thing for a clergyman to preach; it is like Luther, only more radical." But he dislikes the idea of regarding the intelligence of God as the knowledge of our scientists, the kindness of God as our medicine and hospitals. "It is far better to say that the kindness of God is those forces of nature working with man — in other words, Plato's good; because Plato would never identify God with everything, but only with the good. Modern theology is adrift between Plato's idea of the good or God and the old Hebrew idea of God which tends to be pantheistic."

He said he had tried to read Middleton Murry's book on *God*, but could not; and as for Mr. Murry's comparison of D. H. Lawrence with Jesus — "they are as much

alike as Cleopatra and Queen Victoria." Commenting
on Lawrence's story of Jesus, he said: "I don't like
novels about Christ. I never read them. I am not a
believer but I don't like that sort of thing."

He always reads the books of his friend Aldous Hux-
ley as soon as they come out. "Then I know I am up
to date with the latest thing." He had not liked Thomas
Mann's *Death in Venice*, because it was not amusing,
"and if novels are not amusing, why are they written?"
But he appreciates the high seriousness of fiction as expression of the truth of human life. He says, almost like
Proust, that in trying to know things alien to us we reach
nothing but appearance which can be expressed only in
symbols that veil our ignorance, though they may be
useful. Only in relation to minds like our own, which
we reach through what he calls the "literary psy-
chology" of sympathy and imagination, can we arrive
at literal truth.

In 1932 he was working on his own novel as well as
his *Realm of Spirit*. "I'm always writing my novel. It
is a life companion to me and I like it almost too much
to give it up. It is called *The Last Puritan*. I think it
won't be published till after I'm gone, because it might
cause a row. Some of the things I wrote about my colleagues at Harvard made trouble. The scene is laid in
Boston. I got the first three chapters back from the
stenographer the other day and I showed them to Strong
when he was here. Strong didn't like them. 'What
are you trying to do — make fun of these good people?'
he asked me. I thought I was succeeding," Mr. Santayana said, laughing. "When people get old they often
revert to their origin. Strong's father was a Presbyte-
rian minister in a small town. . . .

"In the beginning of my novel the hero is walking along the road on his way to church when he gets a stone in his shoe. Then he has quite a problem: should he take it out or not? If he is taking it out just because it hurts, that is wrong; but if it is really doing him harm, then it should come out. . . . My novel has a sad ending, though. It has to have that. The good young man dies in the war."

In view of the subsequent popularity of his novel it is interesting that he said with regard to the relative popularity of his *Sense of Beauty:* "It is less crotchety than other books on the subject. It is my first book and still my best seller. I think it must be used in a class somewhere because it sells regularly a hundred copies a year. I feel the reverberation in my bank account."

Mr. Santayana is somber and whimsical in his novel, as he is throughout. To the end he will believe: "That life is worth living is the most necessary of assumptions and, were it not assumed, the most impossible of conclusions" (*The Life of Reason,* I, 252). He has written that if nature has fooled us into thinking that it is worse to miss experience altogether than to live a troubled life, "she merely yielded to a tendency to tease which is strangely prevalent among nurses. With a sort of tyrannical fondness, to make us show our paces, she dangled this exciting and unsatisfactory bauble of life before us for a moment, only to laugh at us, and kiss us, and presently lay our head again on her appeasing breast" (*Soliloquies in England,* p. 28).

He simply believes in living as rationally as possible in a world largely irrational. "There is no cure for birth and death save to enjoy the interval" (*ibid.,* p. 97). For him this is the part of wisdom: "To dream with one eye open; to be detached from the world without being hostile to it; to welcome fugitive beauties and pity fugitive sufferings without forgetting for a moment how fugitive they are " (*ibid.*, p. 96).

He seems to know all that is worth knowing, to feel everything that touches the human heart. He writes with the calm of an ancient philosopher, the passion of a mystic poet, the insight into eternal and intimate things which belongs to the great dead. He writes as if he had lived a long time ago and were writing for all time to come.

I I I

The Aesthetic Way of Life

THE NATURE OF THE
AESTHETIC WAY

The aesthetic way of life is the religious way purged of supernaturalism, transcending organization and undulled by routine observance. The beautiful is the divine, free of doubtful promises and unspiritual power. Both religion and science, like all other aspects of life, are cherished by the beauty-lover for their loveliness, and for him require no further authority. He reads the Bible with as much devotion as the devout; feels the sacredness of a holy place as deeply as the faithful; and he worships at the shrine of every human value. Like the mystic he responds to the ineffable in all its manifestations, and while he may be religious in the traditional sense, or seek something like a religious interpretation of his joy, the pilgrim on the aesthetic path finds his all-in-all in beauty, whenever and wherever it appears. For him beauty is enough; it need not point beyond or be vouched for by anything else. What he lives for does not require belief; it is there. He needs only to see and appreciate it. He must love it, and therein lies his fulfillment, for he is the lover of everything lovely.

As the displacement of religion by the materialistic point of view was facilitated by overweening faith in the undeveloped, almost untried, powers of science and technology, so the predominance of the aesthetic attitude will be aided by the manifest failure of both science and religion, after undreamed development, to save the world or alleviate its fundamental troubles. But science will always have aesthetic importance as a source of forms and imagery to be enjoyed in contemplation. Such enjoyment is conspicuous in the case of Marcel Proust. Religion, meanwhile, shorn of gross magic by science, may continue to enrich human life through the pure magic of its poetry. This is the secret of George Santayana, who has shown that as once the faith of our fathers dominated material interests, these may again be mastered by the love of beauty.

People like Proust and Santayana who have discovered contemplation do not envy those absorbed in position and possession, for the aesthetic way of life leads to deeper happiness than the acquisitive way. If men are to give up money-making and power-seeking as their aim they must be converted to the other outlook which involves a transvaluation of values; and if contemplation and aesthetic enjoyment could become popular the Gordian knot in which our social order is tied might be cut. If most people found their joy in goods which cost nothing but appreciation, physical wealth would not be coveted beyond necessity and its fair distribution might no longer be hampered by greed.

The Occidental mind is unlikely to accept the contemplative attitude unless supported by what is called comfort, or at least decency; but Westerners may learn how rewarding contemplation can be. Were their wealth and machinery socialized, and their technologists motivated by love of workmanship and the ideal of constructing a harmonious whole out of the chaos of contemporary society, it might be possible for people in the West to raise their "standard of living." Many Europeans and Americans indeed do endure conditions for them more difficult than similar circumstances would be for Orientals with their inner resources. Western nations must learn how to combine their efficiency with the consolation of Eastern meditation or suffer the increasing evils of competitive industrialism and imperialist war, followed by the probable loss of individual liberty through a communist or fascist dictatorship. Failing such a redemptive fusion, Occidental optimism may lapse into pessimism; more people may question whether life is worth living or promises enough satisfaction in the future to justify their having children.

The aesthetic way of life will not wipe out social injustice; it will not feed the hungry, nor care for sick babies; it will not end labor disputes or international rivalries. But if the technology requisite to secure social justice could be isolated from other interests and pursued exclusively for a time, free speculation, fine art and the amenities of living might later spring up from a firm footing. And if the aesthetic way is neglected pending social reconstruction, man's interest in the arts and the intellectual heritage (except for the strictly scientific) will disappear for ages of darkness while mankind struggles painfully to regain civilization. Meantime, the aesthetic ideal can give point to lives bored by privilege, perhaps to some oppressed by poverty, and to many economically in between. The cultivation of aesthetic pleasure on the part of those susceptible to it may at least hasten a general disillusionment with regard to merely material values.

Elaborate education, extensive travel and other advantages are wasted if they are enjoyed chiefly as spoils of competition and evidence of status. It is the worst kind of waste thus to prostitute the opportunity for more appreciative living; and a person possessed of no obvious good fortune, but who can meditate, may gather from the common run of experience more wisdom and cultivation than is possible to those whose privileges are superficial.

The only hope of a just social order is to shift the valuational center from private profit to private enjoyment of an innocent, inexpensive sort which can be shared and which is enhanced through sharing. To this end people should learn from childhood the joy of contemplation through listening to music, looking at pictures, reading poetry, and dreaming over scenes and feelings in retrospect. What is recalled in reverie has the quality of art, because form in art is wrought of repetition and variation like the rhythm of reminiscence; and to go over experience in memory, as Proust has done, is like following the development of an artistic composition. The aesthetic attitude is not necessarily broken off by present activity, because what is done may be regarded as contributing to the configuration already there. Any undertaking becomes more interesting if it can be regarded in the light of art; and if one's work will not lend itself to this mood, one may in leisure turn to a more soothing and expressive occupation that allows for invention and imagination, whether carving or sewing or only using scissors and paste in making a scrapbook.

The school can help by providing ideas and encouragement. Children should be taught interests that are self-developing and self-rewarding, and nothing should be said about getting better grades than their fellows in order to get better jobs and bigger incomes. Nor should the competitive spirit be allowed to take the subtler form of impelling the individual to read more books, get more information, or think of his fellows as rivals. He should as far as possible be induced to do things and like them for their own sake.

Santayana says that to do away with prizes would make an end of ambition and civilization, unless people became heroes and saints interested in excellence for itself. But, granted that such an interest is heroic or saintly in present society, the question is whether education and environment can be modified to make love of excellence easy and natural. That the experiment is still worth trying, in spite of the discouraging result of education hitherto, must be affirmed unless we are willing to capitulate to money-makers and war-makers. Either a more humane and creative, a gentler and more contemplative way of life must be found or the world will continue to menace anyone with interests which might be called spiritual, moral or intellectual.

Unselfishness is unfeasible so long as men emphasize competition and stress values that one can have only through another's loss. If selfishness disappears it will be because men learn to find their good in being constructive and appreciative, after the manner of the artist and the scientist; though even they may be perverted to invidious, divisive striving since they are human and subject to the valuational trends around them. But art and science are often so liberating to their devotees as to foster a generous spirit even in the atmosphere of an acquisitive society. These pursuits tend to be nobly laissez faire in encouraging each worker to be as original and uninhibited as possible, in the faith that thus human culture will be enriched; and these activities tend to be co-operative on a universal scale. In art and science each individual may profit harmlessly by the achievements of others and all are indebted to the persons who give aid or inspiration — indebted in a releasing manner that contrasts with the burden of financial obligation. Intellectual debt benefits everyone involved, and if its very nature forbids repayment, so much the better.

It is an accident of our economic lack of system that to a large extent the innocently individual and freely co-operative vocations of the artist and scientist seem to rest upon undemocratic privilege or patronage. A more egalitarian society, with a further development of technology, could easily support a wider participation in art and science. Occupants of studios and laboratories tend to be indifferent to the economic structure so long as it permits their work to go on; but they would rejoice if more democratic conditions increased the number of their colleagues. Many people, to be sure, fear that a thoroughgoing collectivism might discredit everything that could not justify itself to the common man, and thus stifle free expression. In any event, it is the duty as well as the joy of creative spirits to work while the light of opportunity lasts — whether the night is coming in which no man shall work, or a brighter day in which more can create. The originative individuals in our society may be establishing a way of life, to be followed in the future, which may be forgotten if they falter; or they may be the last practitioners of what will soon be a lost art and a buried science. If they need justification for persevering, they might equally be honored as the vanguard or the rearguard of a happier race.

Perhaps no such dramatic alternatives are in the balance; life may continue about the same. But today one cannot help feeling that we are at a parting of the ways:

one leading to the destruction of freedom and fineness, the other to peace and beauty. We face the question whether human life is worth continuing, and we cannot avoid moods in which we agree with Santayana that it is doubtful.

Our fathers had religious faith to tide them over this question. Their lives might be sad or sordid and torn by war; but they were spared the tedium of jazzed nerves that abhor silence and forbid contemplation, of movie brains which cannot concentrate. Their religion was not a quaint folkway for students and tourists, but the way of truth and life, to be followed and believed, not something to justify and adjust to science. Instead of film stars they knew the Bible characters, and had characters of their own. Their world was not shriveled with speed, their ears dizzied with noise, their eyes blurred with " ads," their minds dulled with thrills, or their hearts rotted with aphrodisiacs. The comfort of the communion cup is not sipped from thin cocktail glasses, and the mystery of the broken bread does not inhere in dainty appetizers — nor can yawning over the Sunday supplement take the place of reverence for the Last Supper. There is something sacred, however, in the broadcast of a symphony, there are still waters among the " ads," there are retreats from noise and speed; and sensitive souls do pass incognito in the crowd, even though " things are in the saddle and ride mankind " — things that science cannot control — and even though the old religion is alien to many whom it might have comforted. For the *poetry* of science and religion may succeed where their power fails. Art, which the builders rejected as a frivolous or profane ornament, may become the headstone of the corner.

One may ask what chance there is for the aesthetic way to provide a serious alternative to force, exploitation and violence, when traditional religion, with all of its supernatural sanctions, has failed to curb their brutality. The beauty of science and art, the lovely variety that vies with ugliness in the world, the joy of contemplation and quiet creation without thought of reward, will hardly deter men from the lure of power and the use of cruelty when the hope of heaven and the fear of hell did not — unless education can work a miracle!

But perhaps this miracle will occur in spite of the present confusion in the field of educational theory and practice. Most parents have surrendered the guidance of their children, who learn from each other, from the community, from the movies and the masses. And when fathers and mothers retain leadership they are often at a loss what to teach. The question is how they and their children can be in the world and not of it, how they can live without letting the conditions of existence blind them to the values of living. For those who are out of reach of conventional religion, but who yet feel the need of a philosophy, a direction and a hope, the aesthetic way is the answer.

People who have ideals of their own wish their children to be different from that which is normal today, yet not queer; want them to be sensitive and appreciative, but not to suffer. Men and women are not justified in becoming parents unless they believe that life is worth suffering, and that, even at the price of increased suffering, it is best to be as much alive as possible — unlike dead or insensitive things, or mere blind forces and fierce animals unaware of the values which shine for awakened human intelligence. Perhaps no teaching is better than that ascribed by D. H. Lawrence to the Western Indians: "Acknowledge the wonder!"

Some people swallow the universe like a pill, Stevenson said, and they will not be concerned about a way of life, but will simply live without thinking, as if existence were the most natural thing in the world. They seem surprised at nothing, hurt by nothing; nothing pleases them, disappoints or even bores them very much. They are prosaically oblivious of values. Whether this blindness is the result of environment or of temperament, is not clear; though poverty and insecurity surely blunt the appreciation of many values, besides preventing access to them. People who barely have the means of subsistence seldom miss aesthetic goods; but men stultified with material things are equally unqualified for contemplative enjoyment.

Unusually awake to values is Nicolai Hartmann who, in the second volume of his great work on *Ethics*, spreads out a panorama of the value realm, much as Santayana deploys the realm of essence. So many values are simultaneously flashing there that none can justifiably be singled out as a guiding star for action. Almost unaided by value-light, each individual must steer by the uncertain compass of his own fancy and responsibility, according to Hartmann, though for Santayana there is necessity beneath the fluctuations of this compass. Material goods are primary; yet spiritual goods may appeal so much that, while they are attained later, they are first in importance. Fullness of experience and purity exclude each other in Hartmann's scheme, yet each has eternal value. Justice conflicts with love, and love of the near with that of the remote. Neighbor love responds to immediate need, including weakness and sickness; Nietzschean love of the remote treats contemporaries as means to a superior posterity, and hardens the heart to proximate demands. Wherever Hartmann turns his gaze he acknowledges so much absolute value that at the moment of contemplation it seems to be supreme.

But Hartmann does not counsel quietism as a result of the confusion of values which he valiantly fails to marshal in a system. For him many of the most valuable virtues appear " on the back " of actions that do not eventuate as hoped. Intention and effort both have their value regardless of consequences. His strenuous nature would repudiate aestheticism as being a species of Epicureanism, which he rejects as a way of life. Yet he likes the Epicurean emphasis upon awareness of values, and there is nothing in his philosophy (whatever there is in his temperament) to invalidate the aesthetic point of view. Santayana, on the other hand, while he is an aesthete preferring to appreciate and understand, admires men who decide and act. In Santayana as in Hartmann the argument allows for a myriad of dimensions in the value realm and for as many ways of viewing it in the sovereignty of unlimited individual perspectives.

The almost inescapable implication of Hartmann's absolutistic *Ethics*, as of Santayana's relativistic naturalism which practically eschews ethics, is the anarchy of private consciences. T. V. Smith has contended (*Beyond Conscience*) that each man's conscience is right for him, but gives him no right to overrule the conscience of another. Every man, while trusting for himself his own moral feeling, must distrust it as a norm for others, just as he must be suspicious of their commands, especially when they urge violence or pressure, even with the intention of relieving oppression. Santayana has called the attempt to improve other people by force the irony of liberalism. His meaning, however, seems to be that since force is fundamental and can be overcome only by force, it is wise to interfere as little as possible and to make the most of any peace the powers that be allow.

When passions run high it is hard to stand and wait; and the spectator, imagining the feelings of all concerned, is likely to suffer more than participants numbed by the excitement of their effort. But instead of adding to the turmoil of conflicting forces, each embattled in the name of conscience and bearing the standard of some value, it behooves everyone who can to withdraw and contribute the serenity, sympathy and appreciation of a non-combatant, the expiatory suffering of a lover of each side in every conflict, who seeks something victorious in each defeat, something humbling in every victory, something lasting in every passing phase; who is so paralyzed with the horror, mystery and wonder of it all that he cannot move, even when trampled by his infuriated fellows, and can only murmur, " They know not what they do."

We should stop assuming that action is the supreme good to which everything else must contribute. We should not subordinate experiment, speculation and reverie to this ideal. We should explore another way of living, in which action is worth while only as it gives significance to contemplation. Then it might seem absurd to be always joining, organizing, pushing and competing.

Aestheticism is often attacked on the ground of being hedonistic, as if there were something wrong in pleasure

or happiness, which are synonymous to thorough he-
donists and anti-hedonists alike. But the beauty-lover,
though he prefers the joys of contemplation, is like any
pleasure-lover in feeling that the pleasure-despiser must
be a person who finds the hedonic quality more in what
he is ashamed of than in what he is willing to acknowledge among his interests. Nor is hedonism necessarily
egoistic, for the same reasoning or feeling which leads
a man to seek his own greater pleasure may win him to
the ideal of the greatest happiness for other men, vague
as this ideal is, and difficult to work toward without re-
sort to measures that defeat it. If opposition to hedonism
rests on insight into the inevitability of suffering, the
aesthetic hedonist will admit that, like every human
path, his is often paved with pain, but will add that he
enjoys the scenery.

The aesthetic way is already followed not only by
artists and known aesthetes, but by obscure people who
simply love beauty, though they seem to have had scant
effect upon the course of history. How little popular
attraction the aesthetic life has is attested by the prevailing ignorance of Santayana,[1] its most charming expo-
nent. Even his admirers are often disconcerted by the
juxtaposition of pessimism and serenity in the chiaro-
scuro of his personality; for he is happy and harmonious,
yet somber at heart. He is an elusive figure and his
wisdom is oracular. Yet he merely believes in being as
happy as possible in a world like this; feels that a philosopher should be at home anywhere; and doubts whether
reform will increase human happiness unless there is
change from within. He blends Stoicism with Epicureanism, the power to renounce with the capacity to enjoy.

[1] True at least until the publication of his novel.

His aestheticism is tinged with asceticism because he realizes that one must give up many things, but he finds a deep satisfaction in the freedom to contemplate what is left.

To live aesthetically does not involve literally following the example of Santayana or anyone else who has a sense of beauty. It does not require living abroad or in an ivory tower. It does not necessarily mean devoting oneself to the fine arts or to the society of artists; nor does it involve the artificialities often practiced by " aesthetes." Aesthetic is simply appreciative living, with awareness of lights and shadows, textures and tensions. It is living religiously without religion, with a sense of awe and gratitude; with inner joy, in the senses and the mind, in the revelation of the mystery and majesty of the universe; it means welcoming the sun of each succeeding day, the stars of each new night; responding to friends, wondering at their otherness and nearness; and ever marveling at being alive, being oneself, or dreaming.

Action is inevitable, and the West is well aware of its value. The need is not to inhibit action entirely, but to stress contemplation until activity is incidental, until staring at the navel is seen to be no more foolish than going places and doing things without feeling their significance. If umbilicular concentration without overt occupation is empty, vehicular, muscular, or even mental activity without meditation is blind.

Men have to act, and many will indulge ferociously in action; but if more could keep the value heavens in view, the consequent gentleness and tolerance of their spirits would somewhat soften the shocks of conflict. The aesthetic way might draw so many followers that men disposed to prefer the acquisitive, competitive road would realize its futility. But if these rush on to destruction, the values of their trajectories will shine serenely to surviving watchers of the sky. And if, before running their brief course, the doers destroy the dreamers, still the brightness will remain. The stars do not need astronomers; the Milky Way does not have to be trod.

APOLOGY FOR AESTHETES

Proust and Santayana belong, with Schopenhauer, to the great tradition that puts contemplation above action. This tradition has been impugned as aristocratic aloofness by men who stress democratic co-operation in the world's work, but many people are coming to believe that the rush of modern living is redeemed only by moments when they can withdraw into the ancient attitude of the spectator. Like Schopenhauer they find this attitude facilitated by works of art which, in addition to giving pleasure in themselves, give the power of enjoying dramas off the stage, pictures outside frames and music without instruments. Whenever life is already beautiful a person who is developed aesthetically will admire it as a finished masterpiece; and when life is not satisfying he may make it so by seeing it not as it would appear to the casual eye, but as if transformed by the touch of a master.

Aesthetic education is a precious resource for the individual who can avail himself of it while waiting for social reforms slow to come; and when they come, it will be as important as ever, because as they arrive they will be taken for granted and despoiled of their anticipated value, as fast as their novelty wears off. This does not mean that the aesthetic refinement of individuals can be substituted for the efficient organization of society and a Proust or Santayana be run for president. In-

creasing attention should be given to training some people to govern and to educating all people to the nature
and importance of government. If anything like present civilization is to endure, all kinds of technical skill
must be taught. And if this civilization is to prove
worthy of continuance, everyone must have a modicum
of security and comfort. Everyone should be fed,
clothed and housed according to the standard of the
time. Until this is accomplished, artistic culture may
seem a vain thing, except to those who are so selfishly
steeped in it that they see the troubles of their fellows
only as the dark which sets off the light in a picture.
The worst of the actual situation is that people who most
need the solace of beauty are most cut off from it by
worry about grocery bills and rent.

At a time like the present it is hard to see how a person
can be justified in enjoying the aesthetic experience except in so far as he does his share (whatever that is!)
toward mitigating the misery about him. It seems also
that he ought to do what he can to extend his joy to other
people; but there is nothing onerous about this ought,
inasmuch as everyone who loves beauty will wish to
communicate his vision.

With increase of leisure, the development of aesthetic
interest is becoming important for everyone who seeks
finer living. If the majority of people should become
more unfeeling in the general advance of mechanization
and standardization, it would be all the more imperative
for those who remained sensitive to find a way of recon-
ciling themselves to their environment. To a large degree the welfare of the sensitive few is bound up with
that of the population at large. Even aesthetes must be
fed and clothed, and when many people are physically

wretched it may seem outrageous that anyone should demand of life more than material well-being. But if no
one asked more than that, everyone could have at least
that. If the demand for profits and fortunes were given
up, and all learned to be content with modest circumstances, poverty might be wiped out. At least it does
not seem to the aesthete that what he requires beyond a
decent level of living is anything antisocial, anything
that would threaten the welfare of others. He does not
want the opportunity to better himself by worsting his
fellows. The " more " he wants is not a bonus which
would burden the state, but simply leisure.

To him this is not unreasonable, now that he is assured
that science and technology make it possible to reduce
the working hours for everyone to a few a week, and at
the same time to supply adequately the needs of all —
provided that the social order can be revamped to make
this possibility actual. The question is whether the aesthete should feel obliged to work for social reform, or
feel justified in enjoying such leisure as he can get, on
the ground that social injustice is not his fault or his
problem. He may well feel that he is incompetent in
political and economic matters and had better not med-
dle, considering the confusion and helplessness of political scientists and economists themselves, though they
might rejoin that much of their trouble results from the
unhelpful attitude of the public, of which the aesthete
is after all a part.

But there are many kinds of social work from which
he cannot excuse himself through lack of special ability.
What is his duty? He may be moved to devote some
time to relieving misery in any way he can, but how
much time should he set aside for this? However much

he does, since he is sensitive, he may feel that he should do more. He will wish for some way of knowing what his share is; and if he does not draw the line somewhere, he will not only lose all his precious leisure but perhaps health of body and mind, while suffering continues to surge around him. In the end there is only his private, anguished conscience to tell him whether he should keep on trying to sop up a bottomless sea; while the people who appear responsible for it, and who seem in a position to do something effective toward draining it, often act as if it did not exist.

The aesthete may feel that every general social problem should be met by agencies supported by taxes. The burden is too great for the scattered consciences of individuals, whose leisure and peace of mind — which enable them to be individuals — are threatened by the kind of "individualism" that advocates meeting social exigencies through private effort. The individual not only does not know what he should do in the way of social service, but does not know how much money to give, if he has any to spare. As long as other people need money desperately, should he keep even an extra dollar for himself? A conscientious man would gladly be taxed to the limit if then he could feel that at last he had paid off his share of the general burden, and could forget it. This would have been a relief to Proust who was so uncomfortably aware of economic inequality that he always gave fantastic tips.

But if the aesthete is in fairly comfortable circumstances, in refusing to co-operate in active reform he is likely to find himself in the ugly light of benefiting by the evil he will not oppose; and whatever his circumstances, if they allow him to follow the aesthetic way in this world they would be called comfortable by victims of social injustice. Unless he gives up the aesthetic for the ascetic path he will be suspected of collusion with the powers of darkness. It is not strange if he is persuaded of the necessity of action and tempted to throw contemplation to the wind.

Yet his special contribution is the attitude of the onlooker who sees the complexity of the issues, the wrongness of the right and the rightness of the wrong. His distinctive faith is in the development of sympathetic insight into every aspect of experience. His feeling is that action has run amuck and will never erase evil until men have learned to see.

If at no given point can an aesthetic nature say, " Now I have done my stint and may turn to what I really like," his prior values will be diluted with duty, though they need not be entirely lost in a solution of sacrifice. But he cannot lose himself in the group without ceasing to be the individual he wants to be, unless he has faith that his individuality will be returned to him with a dividend of leisure beyond the grave. Perhaps individualism is not worth saving from the point of view of the group, if there is such a point of view. Would-be or might-have-been individuals, whose whole consciousness is concerned with mere subsistence and the avoidance of sheer misery, will not worry about the loss of a luxury like individuality on the part of those whom they regard as pampered. Could-be individuals, those who are economically fortunate, but know not how to spin a web of consciousness refined enough to hold the glittering dew of beauty, will not know what they lack, nor will they pity anyone else for missing it. Once-were individuals, forced by life to part with their birthright, are prone to be equally callous to the loss of it by others. Individuals in the full aesthetic sense may be too few to matter except to themselves, though hidden beneath their protective coloring they may be more numerous than appears.

A main stream would dwindle without tributaries, and human life would be poorer without contributions from remote, snow-high lives. Investigators are excused from participation in ordinary activity because it is believed that their results will benefit action; and artists are let off because they provide diversion that helps men re-enter more vigorously into practical pursuits. The indictment of the aesthete is that he does not intend to heap fuel on the fires of action. But if service is expected of everyone, perhaps the aesthete, in not knowing that he serves, in quietly being himself, serves better than many who bustle or glide about with importance in their manner. As long as men are excused and even honored for taking advantage of the community, apology for aesthetes is easy, except to the spoilers and their admirers; or to reformers and revolutionaries.

Practical people bent on making money, or doing away with money-makers, or helping their victims, are likely to have neither time for beauty nor patience with its lovers, except as beauty can be suborned to profit or propaganda. But exploitation and philanthropy are the rollers of a treadmill. If one can never step off and rest on the platform of aesthetic fulfillment, there is only a phantom profit in success for the few, only a pseudo-salvation in emancipation for the many. If there is excuse for endeavor of any kind, the justification must ultimately be human satisfaction. But no effort can eventuate in fully satisfactory experience without aesthetic appreciation, which is in danger of being lost if not kept alive by aesthetes. Without aesthetic awareness men might as well be ants or elephants. Without it no deed has value; with it, value dawns beyond every achievement.

Freedom to develop the aesthetic attitude is not only pleasant to the individual but vital to the very humanity of the race. While a growing host of experimenters are employed to discover better means of living, it is even more important that a number of men be at least unmolested in the effort to amplify the end of living. New departures are constantly being hailed as discoveries in the realm of processes and devices. Here it is realized that progress does not emerge merely from established procedure, that while rules can be laid down for countless operations, the way to think of something new and better cannot be prescribed. In industry, and every aspect of practice, reluctance to follow old grooves, even when it seems capricious and irresponsible, may bring a richer reward than orthodoxy. And it is truer of goals than of gadgets that necessity is not the mother of invention unless it is the necessity of the mind to be free, to dart out in new directions, to play on the fringe of custom and embroider it with gallant sallies into the unknown.

Everyone who does good work likes it, and no one begrudges this pleasure. If the aesthete's role is socially important, the joy he derives from it is innocent, even if it is private. As T. V. Smith has said (*Beyond Conscience*), pleasure is always private, in the sense of being enjoyed only by the person who has it. When people are said to enjoy the same food, their agreeable sensations of taste and digestion are their own. When they listen to music, read books or look at pictures, each has his own enjoyment, much as it may resemble that of others. So when the aesthete finds pleasure for himself he is not depriving his fellows of a similar satisfaction, especially since it is nourished mainly by nothing more material than an attitude.

Every human good may be interpreted as pleasure, whatever it is — for if no one is pleased by something, what good is it? The aesthete has simply found what poets, saints and philosophers have felt to be the best pleasure — that of contemplation. In the long run his example may be so eloquent that others will cease to denounce or envy, and begin to emulate him. There could be no better society than one in which everyone, by being predominantly contemplative, was so filled with private contentment that he coveted nothing of his neighbor's, and found no lure in power over others, no privilege in commanding or exploiting.

The same body may be the seat of aesthetic appreciation and everyday activity. Artists often betray the wish to be more normal, and the ordinary mortal may occasionally wish to be more artistic. Many a would-be artist might be happier if he could give up his pretensions to being different from other people, while some should cease trying to be normal and be the artists they really are. Public opinion divides between sympathy for artists and antipathy toward their abnormality. Many who would not set up to be aesthetes feel that the artist's function redeems his social deficiencies — that little should be expected of him but his art. His foibles and eccentricities, even his antisocial tendencies, may be forgiven while he continues to sing or paint; and when he can no longer delight, he may be pitied as a fallen angel for whom ordinary work is worse than idleness.

A person with the urge to devote himself to art should be granted the courtesy of hoping that something worth while will come of his efforts, as one grants it to him who has children, before knowing what they may amount to. It cannot be assumed that all would enjoy life more through having a conventional home and children of their own, when the enjoyment of some is in contemplation and expression rather than in possession. An artist may love children without wanting to own any, just as he enjoys places in nature and paintings in a museum without coveting them. Many have felt, with Plato, that it is better to have children like those of Homer and Hesiod than the ordinary kind. So few people know what to do with life except to pass it on, that when a person appears who can enjoy and suffer to the full, who can completely live the life he has, he should be allowed to, and not be made to feel that his duty is procreation rather than appreciation and creation.

The world needs artists and spectators who look on, comment and express, as surely as it needs more participants. But who knows what he should do, once he thinks about it? Rules and definitions blur when they are taken from paper and applied to life — life so amorphous, so volatile and unconfined that whatever men say about it they can never understand it. They can know life only by living, each in his own way, and all together as best they can. They are brought to life without being consulted or warned, and they are no sooner in it than they are hedged with duty and " ought." But if some

can find ways of being free and creative within the limits
they must recognize, that is their privilege and the profit
of all. Only the poets, the artists, the men and women
who feel keenly what it is to be alive, can express the
common lot with its necessities and freedoms, its joy and
wistfulness. Is it not more important that they should
give the meaning of life to the living than that they
should join in swelling the numbers of the living and
the dead?

Aesthetic individuals, on account of their minority
and peculiarity, often feel unhappily that they are mis-
takes of evolution and have no right in a world where
they do not fit, though they feel equally the need of bol-
stering themselves up with the faith that they herald the
emergence or the survival of the highest level of humanity, and that the world really belongs to them. They
have also the comfort of art, which, they feel, speaks
especially to them from kindred spirits. They may read
too much aestheticism into the origins of art and into its
practice in the past; but they can hardly be wrong in
feeling that at least the arts of literature, music and painting at present are the work of people who wish above all
to express their own personal self-consciousness, in order
to escape from the confusion around them into a realm
where they can be at home because it is of their own
making. And everyone who makes a spiritual nest for
himself inspires others to do likewise.

Organized social work sags inevitably into dealing
with types, with the result of missing the special needs
of individuals. Wants which can be effectively met,
through organization and " methods," are those of people *en masse*, though even here there is failure. The
only one who is very successful in touching the indi-

vidual at the quick of his personality is the artist — who can do so because he himself is supremely individual.

One who feels strongly in personal terms apparently cannot help being something of an artist, who will comfort and encourage every individual he reaches. Perhaps here is the answer to the question whether the aesthete should turn to social service or not. The world is stern toward mere aesthetes, yet relatively lenient with artists; and the aesthete is often an artist in the making, who upon becoming an artist will pay his debt to society through rendering personal service to those who need it most. Just as a doctor cannot do his peculiar work without a long training, so the artist cannot make his contribution without apprenticeship as an aesthete. The greater the gift he is to give, the more arduous and devious may be his preparation, the more useless and selfish he may appear, until he succeeds in redeeming himself. The more original and induplicable he is, the harder it will be to judge him, until the gratitude of those who appreciate him begins to illuminate his name, which may not be until after his death, and may be never.

Yet the artist's ability to create beauty is not more ultimate or important than the aesthete's capacity to appreciate it. Art, like life, must be enjoyed to be justified. Save for the appreciative mood in man, and in the aesthete among men, there would be no point to art and no apology for humanity. The aesthete should not feel obliged to give up such leisure as he can enjoy without too much censure — give it up in the same way and to the same degree that one might gladly do who did not prize being alone or feel that his moments to himself were important. Now that idleness is forced on multitudes, and there no longer seems any need for everyone to be continually busy in obvious, overt ways, the individual who feels that privacy is precious should be allowed, and should allow himself, to have it in peace. Instead of anesthetizing himself to his secret happiness, he should be an aesthete unashamed. Were he shameless he would say that but for the moments in which every man is an aesthete, the human race would not be worth saving, would mean no more than fish in the sea or insects in the air can mean to themselves. Human life is not better than any kind of animal life or inorganic existence, except as seen in the mirror of self-consciousness; and the only reason it is worth while to keep people alive is the hope that they or their children may become aware, at least in flashes, of the wonder of awareness.

As far as the aesthete is concerned, social welfare is worth promoting only if it fosters a type of life that is self-conscious, that exists for itself as an end in itself. After all the ages, the poor are still here, and there is no assurance that they will not be with us always, but even they cannot live humanly by bread alone; and unless there is the possibility of living on the aesthetic level, the values in living are wasted. Man is a body without a head if he cannot develop the memory and imagination of the individual, the self-consciousness that is fostered by art. Working in order to eat in order to work, or in order that others may eat to work, is to the aesthete and artist a squandering of time, except in so far as there supervenes a kind of light, to give working and eating and everything else a gleam of value in itself. Only then is the question answered as to what we are living for, unless we can still believe in some transcendental scheme.

While other people go about their business, it is well

not only that a few are producing beauty, but that a few
are admiring it, criticizing, and encouraging its produc-
tion. Nothing cheers an artist so much as the knowledge
that his efforts will be considered with the same loving
attention that he put into them. Though only a minority are appreciative of art their taste should not be
ignored, but should be sheltered and fanned as the spark
of living fire in the heap of humanity. Here is value
that cannot be calculated; and if artists and aesthetes
were to disappear in the future, that would be all the
more reason for their enjoying the experience of beauty
that is open to them now, in a brief eternity. To the
lovers of beauty life is not tolerable without it, and they
cherish for many others the most important values they
can have. Apart from the aesthetic experience, there
may be birth and death, sorrow and rejoicing; but no
appreciation of them, no real feeling for them, no trace,
no echo, no cloud of glory.

To judge exclusively from the aesthetic point of view
would be called the aesthete's fallacy, and, while it is
well for him to assert himself far enough to assure self-
respect, doubtless he should be cautious in measuring all
men by himself. He should be content with having
found, to his own satisfaction, the meaning of life, and
should realize that his own solution will not save people
who lack his insight, though he cannot help hoping and
almost praying for them. Some can put their trust in
science, others in heaven, or they know not what.
Many seem to feel no need of trusting anything; but
many are utterly at sea. To at least some who flounder
the aesthete will throw the life-preserver of art.

His redemptive secret is that to a sensitive soul bereft
of religious faith, even when equipped with science, life

will seem futile unless it can be transmuted into art. Though this is not a salvation for everyone, it will be for some who could be saved in no other way. Few as they may be, the fact that their plight cannot be taken seriously by governments and social agencies makes it fortunate for them that they have recourse to art. A government may even help in remunerating artists and making their work more accessible, and there are aesthetes on relief.

This is the apology for aesthetes: that they appreciate beauty and may become artists; that except for them, men would more often pass on life from generation to generation, and recede into oblivion, not only without knowing but without feeling why.

ARTIST AND AESTHETE

One cannot admire art without admiring artists, and to wonder about it is to wonder about them. The more fascinating a work of art is the more we wish to know what manner of man produced it, how he did it, why he did it, and what his feelings were. People will not accept his work as complete in itself apart from him. They are always grateful to prying biographers, and might welcome the discovery of Shakespeare's life story more than a new Shakespeare play. Many who had not thought of sitting down to the poetry of Shelley or Byron read their biographies with great interest, as people who knew nothing of the Russian ballet and never saw Nijinsky have been entranced with his life.

This might mean that the art of biography is coming to dominate other forms of art; but such an explanation would not account for special interest in the lives of artists, nor for the fact that no one is eager to read portrayals by their Boswells unless they are Johnsons in their own right. Art is still the reason for interest in the creators of art. Even persons who read little poetry feel a mysterious intensity in it, or they would not be drawn to the biography of a poet. Only a person curious about poetry is likely to read the letters of Keats, and one who does read them will scarcely resist turning to his poetry. A reader of Nijinsky's life cannot go back and watch him dance but will wish that he might; and he will cer-

tainly want to see what is left of the Russian ballet. We
wish to find the truth behind art in order better to appreciate art and because we know there will be poetry in
that truth. A work of art is something so individual that
we feel its author must be a person, and one who is really
a person is worth knowing in a world where the odds are
against personality.

It is the nature of the artist to embroider and emboss,
to work over the surface of necessity and give it a need-
less design, a sheen, a finish, or a deliberate roughness
that is pure excess, uncalled for and unexpected, with
no excuse but the delight of doing it and the joy of seeing it. Anyone who takes pride in his work does this
to some extent. He adds something that no one else
would have thought of doing or demanding. This
something is art, whether it appears at the office, in the
home or elsewhere. But the name of artist is reserved
for people who devote themselves professionally to writing or painting or composing, or the like, making original expression not a pleasant addition to otherwise useful
activity, but their whole purpose. The person who is
artistic puts in a gratuitous snap and flourish here and
there like a Negro bootblack; but the artist makes his
whole life a cracking whip, a flag streaming in the breeze.

The essence of a work of art is the vision and feeling
of the artist, his touch and technique, his emphasis and
rhythm. There are schools and traditions of art, there
are classics and standards; but, whatever he learns from
others or shares with them, and much as he may be
rivaled or outdone, the artist enriches human experience
in some unique way, or he is not worthy of fame. His
work must be his signature, something so new that there
is no name for it but his own.

One may ponder the relation between creating and appreciating, between being an artist and an aesthete. The two activities, the two persons, are thought of together and are often one, yet they are separable and may be opposed. It is common knowledge that the appreciator may lack creative ability, but it is also true that the creative nature may be lacking in taste and vision. Persons regarded as sensitive and critical (and they constitute the only bar of aesthetic criticism) are constantly surprised to find what men and works a great artist admires. Van Gogh liked painters considered to have little merit and none of his qualities; Robinson Jeffers is said to enjoy reading anything that is literate; and the artist is often so self-sufficient that any stimulus will serve. The uncreative appreciator wants to contemplate finality; but the artist works over everything that comes his way. The perfect and the weak, the awkward and the graceful, are grist for his mill, as if he saw not what was there but something within that strikes sparks on everything without.

The aesthete may be more intellectual, more conscious of what he likes and what distinguishes it from what he dislikes, while the artist is driven by an unconscious urge and creates because he must, without caring where he is going. The appreciator tends to look back toward what is settled, labeled and ranked; the creator goes beyond landmarks to stake out new claims. If the artist were more discriminating he might be more deferential, more fearful of tradition, less free to strike out for himself. If Dickens had seen his work with the eyes of a critic and had been horrified by what are called his lapses of taste, he might not have pushed on to the passages generally admired. A person will certainly respond

most to the artist whose taste he can upon the whole accept, but will have to admit artistic ability, in the sense
of power to mold a medium and make it expressive, even
in the case of many works he would call ugly.   An artist
is like nature, which makes caverns and crystals, insects
and sunsets, dreams and diseases.   He makes what he can,
because he must, like the beaver or the bee.

The artist may pause to take the aesthetic attitude toward his work before it is finished and to get cues for its
further development; when it is done he may enjoy con-
templating it; but his peculiar pleasure as an artist is in
forging new forms, rather than in basking in old ones.
While an admirer may repeatedly go back to past
achievements, discovering in them new glories, the artist
himself is often indifferent to his finished works, delight-
ing more in making something new out of old impressions and expressions fused with fresh experience and
insight.   In this fundamental respect the artist tends not
to be an aesthete.

On the other hand, as is obvious in the case of Proust,
being an aesthete may be the first step toward becoming
an artist.   To appreciate beauty engenders a longing to
express it, if only in exclamations, and one can improve
on their inadequacy only by being artistic.   To respond
to another's art is to feel the answering throb of one's
own creativity, and, the more wonderful art seems, the
more urgency one may feel to become an artist, if the
feeling is not stifled by fear or incapacity.   To a considerable degree artistic ability depends upon confidence; Otto Rank may be right that a person must deliberately appoint himself to the artist-type, must make
himself his first work of art.   The necessary soul-search-
ing in our society may be very strenuous, because we do

not accept art and artists as natural phenomena, except as freaks and geniuses are natural. It takes courage for an art-lover to think of himself as he thinks of genius, while realizing how other people regard a self-appointed genius who has not established himself as one. To think of himself as a dabbler would be more modest, but would be fatal to his dream. Not only is our society contemptuous of dilettantism, except for young ladies waiting to get married, but the aesthete who loves art passionately feels that to play around the edges of the real thing is worse than nothing. So the aspirant to creation goes up and down on waves of hope and despair, tossed between the dread alternatives of all or nothing.

His trouble is aggravated by the absence of any objective way of knowing whether he is deluded in his ambition or in his self-distrust. He may think that if he could borrow a reputation the recognition of his work might be immediate, but, knowing how indiscriminate and softening popularity is, he may be thankful for decent obscurity, except that as long as he is unknown it is hard for him to know whether perseverance is sincere or silly. That the incipient artist will find food and drink in the encouragement of an established artist or aesthete might indicate that, apart from the applause and disapproval of the crowd, there are standards in art and experts who know them. But what they know is after all their own feeling, and who the knowing are, each must feel for himself. The true artist will keep on undismayed by the most knowing — but so may the hopeless, would-be artist.

And why should he not, if he is psychologically, physically and financially able? The would-be artist may be as happy as, and no more unhappy than, the real artist,

and nothing will ever decide with final objectivity
which is which. Popularity cannot settle such a question, nor authority, nor the feeling of an individual, except for himself. And the world might be better off
with more people trying to be artists and fewer trying
to be wealthy or powerful. The main question for the
artist (good or bad) is whether he is able to keep on
trying to be one; whether he is able to sacrifice sufficiently. The aesthete risks comparatively little and
need not materially alter his way of life to make room
for appreciation — except as he risks wanting to be an
artist who is characterized by readiness to lay everything on the altar of art. But to remain an aesthete may
be compensation for inability to become an artist.

Since success and failure in art are practically in-
distinguishable, and elude impartial, objective judgment,
the artist's attitude is all-important, his sincerity is
everything. Not only must he believe in himself even
when no one else does, but he must ever strive to do his
best on his own responsibility. He cannot be externally
held to established standards, for his gift is unique and
can be estimated only in terms of itself. His sole obligation is to do what he alone can, and his own integrity
is the only guarantee of that.

With objectivity out of the question in art, subjec-
tivity reigns supreme — the artist's attitude as sensed by
others. In the absence of a tangible, unequivocal test
of his achievement there is a temptation for him to cheat,
to pose and pretend instead of making a genuine effort;
and there is a corresponding pitfall for the observer in
the danger of making believe that he perceives a work
in a certain way instead of relying upon his actual feeling about it, however vague. Art is a realm so charged

with emotion and suggestion that it is easy for creator and appreciator alike to become confused, and the only safeguard for either is sincerity. The possession of it is as precious as the lack of it is serious. As justice and right-eousness shine by their own light, regardless of results, so, as Nicolai Hartmann might say, artistic sincerity has its own value independent of what is called success — is indeed a kind of success that no failure can blemish. The poor musician in Grillparzer's story, though he played atrociously, to the narrator's ear, was absolutely consecrated to his art as if he were the greatest artist on earth. But greatness is a matter of opinion; sincerity exists in itself and elicits admiration from everyone, apart from the quality of the external accomplishment.

Dedication to art is sometimes explained as compen-sation for failure to participate satisfactorily in normal living; but whatever truth there is in this the artist is a person for whom ordinary existence could never take the place of art. He tends to regard life as only the ma-terial and stimulus for art, if not a dangerous distraction to be shunned. In Thomas Mann's *Königliche Hoheit*, Martini, the poet, says: " Renunciation is our pact with the Muse: thereupon depends our strength, our dignity; and life is our forbidden garden, our great temptation, to which we succumb occasionally, but never to our benefit." He lives sparingly, anxiously, saving himself for his art. However reckless and debonair an artist may appear in his work, he is likely to live with the regularity of a *petit bourgeois*, as Matthew Josephson shows in his biography of Zola; while Cabell, in *Beyond Life*, presents poetry as so antithetic to life that if poets do not die young they usually cease to be poets. An art-ist will avoid drains on his energy and may refuse to take chances that others think nothing of, because he has projects so important that they make him indifferent to the figure he cuts before convention. He does not mind being thought queer, because he knows he is more queer than anyone would suspect. He is glad to appear stupid if it saves him from clever people; and he may rejoice in being impossible to nice people. The world may say he is not an artist, but if it will let him *be* one he does not care. All he asks is freedom to work.

In *Königliche Hoheit* the artist is symbolized by the royal prince living in the remote formality of the palace but wistful about normal existence, envying uninhibited people who live freely. In *Tonio Kröger* Thomas Mann shows how the artist is forced to stand aside from life while needing to participate; for the artist requires vitality as much as he craves form. And in *Peter Schlemihl's Wundersame Geschichte* by Chamisso, which Mann has pondered, the hero is ignominiously bereft of his shadow, the symbol of decent solidity, in exchange for unnatural wealth, the gift of poetry.

The artist must have an animal footing and a human feeling. It is well if he can be a healthy animal, because human emotion is a strain on an organism, and to make the same organism also an instrument of expression is dangerous. The artist is like a circus performer standing on the shoulders of a man on a horse. His balancing act requires equine power and human skill, all in one, and the difficulty of co-ordinating them makes it easy to explain failure, while success can only mean training and practice. The more daring the stunt the more dull the preparation, the more persistent and conscientious it must be. The regimen of an acrobat's life would soon bore the people who watch him open-mouthed. It is seldom the star-performers in any art who deliberately dissipate their energy and play the Bohemian. They know that to defy the limitations of life they must first submit.

Work is the artist's conscience; work is his only duty and his whole reward. He will do without money if necessary and possible, though money is precious because it means time to work, a place to work in, privacy and independence, honesty, and a promise that he can finish what he has begun — and begin again. He will do without fame, knowing who have done without it before and who receive it now, though recognition is sweet and a vindication. He will do without friends, but he needs a few to keep up his courage and to comfort him in the loneliness of his work. He needs them to love, for he is very much alone.

Only by breaking over the accepted and the expected can the artist pass beyond mediocrity. But the way of the transgressor is hard. He may be admired but he is sure to be misunderstood, and likely to be miserable. Short of becoming a hermit he is forced to have commerce with uncongenial spirits, but this so wears on him that he pants for privacy and soon retreats to his own abode. When he emerges he will go in disguise, dressing and acting inconspicuously, and will be thankful for every opportunity to withdraw into himself. By a kind of freemasonry he may find his own sort here and there among the multitude of others. A few sympathetic friends will mean more to him than glory, but he cannot count on either. He cannot have easy relations with humanity except by ceasing to be himself, for dislike of the unlike holds in society as in the barnyard; and, whatever else he is, the artist is different. When a convenience intended for the public happens to fit a need of his, he feels like a dwarf or giant who finds that a store carries his size in stock; and when a general entertainment pleases him it is as though natives in the streets of a foreign city were suddenly to speak his mother tongue. The necessity of getting along with other people forces him to learn another language and to lead a double life; when he is alone or safe with kindred spirits he is as far from the world as a Christian in the catacombs.

But he is related to the heathen around him and feels the old Adam in himself; and in drawing aside to follow his art the artist hopes to express something deep enough to be common to all mankind. Expression may so absorb him as to become an end in itself; but any unbiased biography will reveal the duality of his character and the struggle he underwent to maintain a balance between the demands of humanity and art. The spur of expression is the tension between man and artist in the same person. If the artist could put off humanity to be a mere craftsman his art would miss fire; and if he could become a well-adjusted normal citizen the incentive to creation would be stifled.

Artist and aesthete alike may be distrusted by the average man who is uncomfortable in the presence of valuations alien to his own. The normal person is taken up with living according to current opportunities and motives, while artists are absorbed in the expression of living. He cannot live without expressing himself somewhat, however informally; and they can neither express nor appreciate a representation of existence without having lived, however ineffectually or unhappily. They cannot help being fascinated by him as the pivot of all their fancies; while he will have moods at least

in which he is moved by the recognition of his realities
in their forms. The activities, settings and surround-
ings, the patterns and perspectives, the emotions and at-
titudes of human life provide all the motives of art. The
beauty of art is simply the acknowledgment and enhancement of what is valuable in life. In so far as art
and life are at variance there is a serious dislocation in
our civilization. Either the artists are not expressing
what is fundamental or people are not living in accord-
ance with basic values, or both. Whether this is owing
to a temporary or permanent human perversity, it is hard
to say. The artist's expression of life today tends to be
an indictment; while the man uncritically committed to
the prevailing way of life resents the critique implicit in
the artist's approach and the aesthete's approval of it.

Artist and aesthete stand together against the inartistic
and unaesthetic, but they differ in orientation. One is
essentially active, the other dominantly contemplative.
Art and life spur the artist to further effort; the more he
admires the more impatient he is to create. The pure
aesthete is content to look on, note and compare, and
in everything acknowledge the wonder. He feels an
obligation to observe and absorb all he can, and nothing
gives him more pleasure. He may be more receptive
than the artist, more leisurely, more an amateur and con-
noisseur of the qualities around him; and may be happier. What he appreciates delights him without arousing envy or despair, unless he wants to be an artist, or is
a professional critic with a reputation to defend. The
artist is likely to notice only enough to give him an im-
petus or renew it; he is blinded by his own light, though
that illumination may be powerful enough to achieve
something like what Schopenhauer called the complete

objectivity of genius, the transcendence of individuality, and the quality that Proust called being a mirror.

The aesthete might be considered more unselfish, generous, modest; but the artist's virtue is that of being creative; he finds his pleasure in doing and giving, enriching the world. Schopenhauer said that only a genius, a creative artist, could really appreciate the work of genius. Proust and Croce agree; but on the contrary, the artist as such may lack the time, the patience, the inclination to appreciate the works of other men as the aesthete does, the person who has no pictures to paint, no books of his own to write, but only a passion to enjoy those of others.

Whether it is better to be an artist or an aesthete is a futile question; and one cannot say which the world needs more. In ancient Greece the perception of beauty was accounted higher than the creation of it, because beauty was regarded as something uncreated and eternal that could at most only be imitated by man; and if the imitation was done by hand, as in sculpture or architecture, it was menial labor. The modern romantic glorification of the artist has turned the tables, so that now imitation does not compare with expression and appreciation is ranked considerably below creation. It is thought better to do than to know, and mere knowers (unless their knowledge is pure and unenvious) may fear that they do not feel as keenly as the doer or they would be able to do likewise. Perception is made ancillary to feeling attested by performance. But in any full philosophy knowing, feeling and doing all go together so indissolubly that where one is present, there are the others also.

The artist's work is not essentially different from that of any workman, unless it is especially intelligent and sensitive, unless it springs from insight and soars to vision. The material art object and the physical process of making it are instrumental to the imaginative enhancement of life. Were the work done mechanically, and never perceived by anyone with a quickened pulse, there would be no aesthetic value. Art excites the beholder because he feels that he is responding to feeling; and the artist is excited by the conviction that his feeling will arouse an answering emotion.

Aesthetic effects are always affective; the artist's labor begins and ends in sympathetic perception; the aesthete's response is the inspiration and the chief reward of art, beyond the hypnotic satisfaction that intense effort carries in itself. The appropriate fulfillment of Proust's work was its being read by Santayana. At the same time it is the artist's work which gives the aesthete his most precious experience. It is characteristic of Santayana that he should have enjoyed Proust.

The artist may be isolated by the effort to express what all men share. But some men, in their off-moments, will stop to admire his performance, and when they go back to work his rhythms and images will stay with them, like ticket-stubs in their pockets, to remind them of his interpretation and intensification of life. When the artist succeeds he comes as close to them as their own souls. When he calls to them from the depths of his own being they are drawn to him from the bottom of theirs, and his oddity is overlooked. Later it is forgotten and he is loved as the most human of all.

To appreciate a work of art is to feel the pulse of another personality. No one else could have done what the artist has done, for it is clearly and mysteriously his own; yet when men respond to his work it moves them, reverberates through them and makes them yearn for expression. But his performance no sooner stirs them to express something deep within them than they realize that he has spoken for them, has written or composed or painted what they feel, and that they are won to him because they are one with him. When they discover that all his admirers share their feeling, it is a tremendous secret among them. The strange thing is that after being made highly self-conscious, through finding how a work fits them and how fully they can live in it, they should learn that others have the same experience. Yet this is not so strange as realizing that some people do not respond as they do. They can explain this only by assuming that the others have not really felt it or by admitting that they are different.

The difference between the artist and other men is that while living is enough for them, he wants to express what it is to live, the fun and the sting of it. He is not engaged in a stupid duplication of existence, but lights up human lives with his sense of humor and tragedy, his power to reach the pith of experience, to remember trifles in a way to make them tremendous, and to reduce a confusion of impressions to a searing simplicity. He comments and interprets, ministering to the deep human craving for a human rendering of the universe. The absolute truth would be colder and remoter than the stars without an intervening veil of art through which men could pick out constellations and make comparisons and analogies in symbols of familiar import. If men could reach a stark in-itselfness of the cosmos they could only stare at it.

As men in some moods personify nature and are delighted by an echo, the artist idealizes an audience and

imagines a response; with the difference that the an-
thropomorphic attitude toward nature may be a pathetic
fallacy, whereas the artist's charitable impulse toward
the public may rest on a pathetic truth. He feels that
beneath the division between him and others there is a
bond; that what he has to express will strike a responsive
chord; because the only distinction between him and
them is that he can intensify and interpret a common
experience. For him it is lighted by his insight; for
them it is still in the dark; but the purpose of his work is
to dispel that darkness.

In man alone, so far as we can tell, the universe comes
to consciousness. Man alone is aware that there is a universe, that it has a history and may have a destiny. Man
is the only spectator in the theater of eternity. Only for
him is the endless drama played; only for him is there
doom or deliverance. But man is not man except in
imagination, and is most human in the sensibility of the
artist; for he is most aware and feels most fiercely the
adventure of awareness. The high-water mark of evolution is the most intense self-consciousness, and this is
achieved by extreme variants of the human species, by
freaks and misfits: men who are sometimes insane, often
psychopathic and always queer.

The queerest thing in the world is consciousness, and
humanity itself is a sport of nature in not only being but
being aware. Anything else just is: if it also has feeling
or intelligence, it simply has it without feeling that it
feels or knowing that it knows. The difference is that
a man not only reacts to individuals and situations but
responds to his responses through gestures that have
meaning in the significant sense of the word, because his
gestures point out to himself what they indicate to others.

A man's behavior is not only there for others but for himself, and since it is there for himself he can correct or develop it, and he can enjoy it.   Other animals are only actors, or if they are also observers they observe only one another.   A man is a true spectator because he watches his own performance, and also because he can see that he is watching the antics of others.   This makes it possible for him to communicate with his fellows in a new way; not as ants do, without knowing that they do it, but as men do who understand what they are saying.   Because men are able to eavesdrop on their own conversation with others, they can talk to themselves. George Herbert Mead, who developed this view of consciousness, said that man is the animal who can call on himself and find himself at home.

This capacity to use gestures or symbols in a significant way with others and with himself has enabled man to outstrip all his rivals, and tell about it.   But as humanity is to the rest of creation, the artist is to other men. Compared with him they are inarticulate and uncommunicative.   They may be alert and active; they may have moments of illumination that move them to private or open comment; and for hours at a time they may join others in a simian stimulation of vocal reflexes; but in comparison with the artist they have nothing to say, no self to commune with and no appreciation of the selves in other people.

The artist stirs the rest of mankind to realize the strange kinship of the species; the weird brotherhood of beings who not only breed and die but look before and after; who know their own nature and transcend it in the knowing; who know the airiness of life and the emptiness of death; who breathe not only to live but to speak; whose breath gives all things their names, their laws and their value, in a vapor of words, a veil of good and evil floating over all the earth and reaching to the stars; hiding and revealing the animal in man, the human in man; a mist of words creating and defeating his genius; a cloud of ambiguous, equivocal words discovering verity, obscuring vanity; a steam of syllables and sentences, prayers and blasphemies, inventing or destroying cosmologies and gods; nothing but words reducing or raising everything to words, in the respiration of *homo sapiens.*

Words are in everyone's mouth but on few people's minds after the first wonder wears off, except for crossword puzzles. Rhymes and fairy tales delight childhood; philosophy fascinates adolescence. But civilized men, when they grow up, put away poetry and metaphysics with childish things, and give up mystery for mystery stories; they settle down to duties and debts and forget their dreams. In a world staled by custom a man who will not surrender his vision is rare. He is refreshing in the midst of boredom and business. He is an aesthete or an artist.

An artist works with words and plays with them. He sees their meaning and hears their music. He knows that words are symbols and that symbols are not merely spoken or written, but chiseled and wrought in many ways. He can make stone as eloquent as air; he can make walls speak and the ceiling sing. He can strike sparks from men, even men in the seats of power, fixed in their inertia and hard as iron: they will ring to the hammer-blows of imagination.

Huddled on the deck of the world humanity is adrift in the infinite. There come dark watches when brave men are afraid, wise men are baffled, and all men are grateful for a song or a story to relieve the monotony and comfort the heart. Best is a long story or an endless song, on a voyage that will never end, on a ship that has no home port and no harbor ahead, no sailing orders, no course but its own wake, no pilot and no steering wheel, no life-boat, no name on the bow and no name on the stern. The passengers cannot keep busy or sleep all the time; they cannot be loving or quarreling continually; and few can amuse themselves. But the artists aboard can make life bearable with their fables and tunes, their rhythms and images. Artists can while away the hours and make men forget their plight, or cause them to feel a sustaining harmony beneath the keel and a purpose at the prow.

THE AESTHETIC RETREAT

The path to beauty may be a retreat from living and not an advance into the press of life, because appreciation is favored by withdrawal, though not necessarily by inaction or laziness. Strenuous activity offers as much for contemplation as quiet hours if time and the mood for realization can be found. But leisure is more conducive to the dreamy detachment of the aesthetic attitude; though dreaming may inspire redoubled activity in art, and even in practical projects, as with many mystics. Whether plunged into intermittently or indulged in habitually, the aesthetic or contemplative quality implies a spectator standing aside to look on, or look back, for values have a trick of lighting up in retrospect.

The aesthetic temperament is likely to be childless, because instead of begetting new experience it tends to linger under the paternal roof of the past — cold to the warm advances of the future and Platonically in love with eternity. Unlike religion which promises another world, and communism which promises this one, aesthetic salvation is in the imagination, and so is more or less incompatible with interest in controlling and continuing existence. The consistent aesthete like Santayana, while revering the vital roots of his being, seeks fruition on the plane of essence where he finds the unfading form of his desire.

Perhaps only a philosopher can appreciate the aesthetic possibilities in life without committing himself to it altogether. His insight merely corroborates and elaborates the wisdom bought with common experience, but most people appreciate only what they seek in fact and know in the flesh; what they work or suffer for, and lose. When they are bereft memory and dreams may teach them the eternity of essence, wherein no lovely thing is lost because there it was never born and cannot die.

Overcome by wonder already haunting the world, the aesthete or artist may not be eager for progress, though like Nietzsche he may be fired with the vision of supermen to come. He is characteristically lonely but may love his fellow men, like Walt Whitman. He is often unmarried, yet may be a *pater familias* and become lyrical over a child, like Thomas Mann.[1] He is often at odds with morality, yet may celebrate the nobility of common duty and loyalty, like Joseph Conrad. He may even be heroic in action, like Lawrence of Arabia; though Lawrence felt remorsefully that the betrayal of the Arabs by his government was his punishment for leaving his proper sphere of contemplation for the practical world where he knew achievement was equivocal.

The aesthete's skepticism about participation need not hurry him to suicide, since he is ascetic only to keep his joy pure. He does not deny the values of life at large or in fine. He respects existence as the condition of contemplation and is aware, or may be, that ideal forms appeal to him through a natural basis in his organism and personality. He can share the naïve satisfactions of normal men, though they do not understand his renuncia-

---

[1] Cf. his *Gesang vom Kindchen*.

tions or at all see what he has left. But he is prone to hold back where others rush in, often because he is afraid of hurting them as well as himself. And if he does not have children the reason may not be selfishness but hesitation to pass loved ones the poisoned cup of life while he lingers in fascination at Belshazzar's feast, after the moving finger has written on the wall.

"To be or not to be" is surely the unreal problem of a dreamer or aesthete, because it is practically settled for everyone by the fact of birth, as Santayana has remarked; but, applied to the future existence of the race, Hamlet's question need not be rhetorical. It has a genuine answer in voluntary parentage, which may become a watershed between lovers of wisdom and lovers of children, though the latter are not unwise nor the former devoid of tenderness. The continuity of the generations is a thread easily snapped, which cannot be tied again save by a decision difficult to make; for if it is criminal to end another's life, to launch it may be equally serious, since a death is implicit in every birth. But if cutting off or initiating an individual existence is a grave matter, to be an accomplice in the annihilation of the race cannot be taken lightly. Yet no less is involved in the aesthetic attitude when it spreads to sex, which, when severed from former consequences and enjoyed for its intrinsic value, may seal up human life instead of endlessly renewing it.

After observing the evil inherent in existence a sympathetic person may shrink from disturbing his presumptive children in the untroubled sleep of non-being. Were they merely asleep upstairs he might hesitate to wake them, even to see the *aurora borealis;* and he knows that if they awake to life, it will be to poverty and war, disease and disillusion.   An ancient Hebrew could have twelve sons to fight for the Lord, but a modern son will fight for a standard of living or to save civilization for later wars; and if he escapes war he can scarcely avoid a desperate struggle with futility.   No one can survey the condition of mankind without shuddering at the ills his flesh would be heir to.   Happiness cannot be denied, and joy and ecstasy, but can these outweigh the certainty of suffering?   Lamb, in his loneliness, should have been comforted that his dream children were safe from the nightmares of reality.

To seek satisfaction in parenthood may be unfairly treating children as means to an end, and the end may not be attained.   So much comes between the generations in the close quarters of the home that they must hurt each other and are lucky if they do not hate each other. Mole hills easily become mountains where special kindness is expected; where an inadvertence is a slight, and every slight a grievance; where the wish of each tends to be the obligation of all, and intimacy precludes the excuse of ignorance.   Children deprive their parents of opportunities as surely as they contribute to their experience, and may be ungrateful for the boon of life in seemingly fortunate circumstances.   Overhanging universal insecurity, the home may be a nest of vexation where even the love of lovers dies instead of being strengthened by the bond of children, who in their turn must pass on the baleful torch or hold it until it gutters out.

Fearful to leave the earth that held his cradle, a man may want a child to bear his name and stamp his features on the future.   But there are other ways of achieving gradual oblivion, ways in which it is easier to make a name stand for what it should; for there is no knowing what disgrace or doubtful honor will deck a family tree not trimmed in season. Nor are offspring certain to improve the morals of their author, making him more tender or altruistic, since affection and anxiety for his own brood can very well absorb a man's generosity for other men. It is hard to be a father and a philanthropist, as Plato and the Catholic church have known. Great benefactors of mankind have seldom been responsible for a family, though they have often been neglectful of one.

Even with the balm of beauty a human being can be lost in the night of the soul like a child in the dark, yet know that but for something like the grace of God he would have been in worse case, and no one knows what is to come. If human life can but persist long enough it may become more definitely worth while for posterity; though in view of the endless ages that have elapsed one might expect more improvement to have occurred, if it were a matter of time — streaming against the windshield of the present and receding in the little mirror pointing to the rear. We are poised between infinites fore and aft, with no objective way of gauging whether life was ever worse or will ever be better. The smile of nature dispels morbid thoughts even in the minds of those who profess to love art more than life. They too may respond to the tug of flesh, and find the way of it as rich in aesthetic possibilities as a visionary road. But no thoughtful person believes that existence is always worth having, or that the creation of more lives is necessarily a good.

Voluntary parentage might become more momentous in the record of the race than the use of fire, the domestication of animals, the adoption of agriculture, the invention of writing, or the industrial revolution. Men accept the inevitable, but when they have the power of choice they question, especially in affairs of life and death; and the exercise of intelligence, in its imaginative reaches, if it cannot solve fundamental problems, can lift humanity above them. Caught in the vise of universal nature every living thing grows and decays; and so it may be, not only with individual men but with their kind. Size, strength and heavy armor protected for a while, then doomed the dinosaur. Rocks crack by their own hardness; mountains fall by their own weight, and by the invisible will of heat and cold, or the sinister caress of water. Cleverness is ultimately clumsy, its brittleness is not impervious to time; but imagination can lay hold on eternity.

That our type of life, or life at all, is better than its absence is a boast that may have nothing back of it but egoism; and if we try further to demonstrate the supremacy of our species in the struggle for existence, the termites may shame us in the end, since they fight their enemies while we fight one another. The justification of replenishing the earth with our breed may be doubted when the most scrupulous person not only treads on other forms of life but lives more or less at the expense of other men. The food he eats, the clothes he wears, the position he holds, he usually takes from another; not to mention the fine psychological ways in which he cannot avoid hurting his fellows. And if our race should one day reach the point of not feeling malice or envy, would it still be human? The travail involved in attaining that anesthetic condition would have no human advantage if humanity ceased to be except in the realm of essence, where man would remain a metaphysical possibility that once happened to be exemplified on the plane of existence. Evolution beyond evil would do away with such as we no less efficaciously than race suicide. Having already won, to our own satisfaction, the highest honors of nature, perhaps we should withdraw from competition and be henceforth *hors concours*.

Earthly survival is an insect's triumph compared to the human opportunity of following in the train of Socrates, Jesus, Buddha and all who have renounced mere living for the sake of an ideal beyond life and death. Not only holy men, but many men have had the tragic sense that self-conscious existence must be expiated. The brutes, even when red in tooth and claw, live in the innocence of paradise, but man cannot avoid a feeling of guilt in so far as he is sensitive and tries to be righteous; and he may not always be so romantic as to prefer tragedy to surcease. Moralists may say that happiness is not what human life is for, but few people would care to have children if their happiness were irrelevant. If not the enjoyment of life, but suffering, heroism or loyalty is the end of man, there are those who will hate suffering, regret heroism when it is tragic, despise it when theatrical, and conscientiously object to continuing an existence whose highest value is sheer allegiance. Reflective beings must reason why, with regard to doing and dying, or be like children unable to stop swinging when tired, though it would be a relief " to let the old cat die."

Evolution has had a long climb up to man, who alone of all creation asks whether it is worth while to go on. As Schopenhauer said, man is the turning point of the will; and in the voluntary rejection of parentage he has a weapon with which he might extinguish the race. He

has the opportunity to reduce his existence to a metaphysical essence as pure and painless as any in the realm
of possibility. Thus might deliverance be achieved for
all the children of man. Thus might they be as angels
in heaven, and paradise never again be lost. So might
come the kingdom not of this world, the house of many
mansions; in a consummation not coming in an outward
manner that could be observed, because it would be
within the inmost recess of being. This might be the
glorious close of evolution, in which man would have
grown beyond growth to find eternal rest.

The passing of man from the realm of existence would
leave a wake of buildings soon to fall and crumble like
his bones, while he was forgotten save for the momentary loneliness of a few deserted pets. With his going
this would cease to be a vale of tears. Death would continue to stalk the earth, but without a shadow. If another species should ever eat of the fruit of the tree of
knowledge and inherit the curse of Adam, a new humanity in its turn might learn to lay aside existence and
find salvation in escape from the wheel of birth and re-
birth. By purging itself of intelligence the world might
shake off time and pain and return to Nirvana.

The human race could commit suicide as gracefully
as an old Roman, lulled by the last refinements of civilization as by sweet music; and if man has drunk existence to the dregs he should be ready to go. The dream
of progress may be over, now that we fear we are not
better than our fathers. Instead of an endless escalator
rising to Utopia, we may see again before us the oval
track of Olympia, curving back on itself. Having run
the course, we may have won and lost all there is to win,
except release. We thought with science to conquer

pain; with democracy to end injustice; with education to abolish ignorance. But now we are not sure that life is richer, the future brighter. We continue to have wars and rumors of wars; and the making of books is still a weariness to the flesh. History is a parade of nations pioneering like our own; fighting for power and succumbing to defeat or victory. Archeology uncovers dead cities of the past that we may behold in them our pride and our shame. We see that our ancestors also had diseases and ideas. They had no motor cars, airplanes or telephones, but they had toys as pretty and as terrible as these. They had all that matters to us; and can we even add to what they have said on the eternal themes?

But it may be overweening for us to assume the power or the right to deny the will to live. Much as we weary, there is still the chance that instead of marking time we are climbing cosmic steps; and that if we stop, thinking we have reached the summit, we may fail to see even from afar the promised land. We have not heard the last trump blow. With our vaunted gift of looking before and after we are cooped up in an everlasting now, as if the past and future were murals on the cell of the present; so that if we had children all might be the same with them as it was with us.

The only good reason for having children is to have them for their own sake, in the hope that with a fresh start they might find life better than their parents did, or at least as good. They might rejoice in it despite the pain, as we have; and if they could not bear it they could give it up; whereas unborn they would have no choice. They cannot follow the aesthetic way if all roads are barred.

The aesthetic attitude might seem an ironic fulfillment, if in bringing appreciation it brought the efface-
ment of awareness. But while existence is the future of
souls waiting to be born, death is the end of life, and it
may be well for the living to make it their goal. " Nature has marked out the path for us beforehand; there
are snares in it, but also primroses, and it leads to peace." [1]

[1] From Santayana's essay on " A Long Way Round to Nirvana," in
Some Turns of Thought in Modern Philosophy, p. 101.

TWO VIEWS OF ART

The aesthetic retreat from life leads toward the ivory tower whose occupants [1] assert that aesthetic experience is not a natural human function but an esoteric affair, having nothing to do with the market place or the commonplace. In this view beauty is confined to art, and art is mysterious. In this view women are never beautiful, nor moonlight, nor mountains. To ascribe beauty to things outside art is merely a way of saying that one likes them, that they are pleasing to the natural or practical man. Art is said to appeal to a different man, an inward man, who has no traffic with this world, a stranger except in the heaven of art.

The aura of traditional religion is about this cult of art. No ascetic could be more acid in denunciation of the flesh and its pleasures than aesthetes who preach the gospel of art undefiled by natural delight. They scorn what the unwarned, unawakened person would regard as satisfactory experience. Interests which he would think entirely innocent, they find steeped in sin, the sin of unsophistication. The man who is still unredeemed goes on loving women, liking food, money and comfort, and even speaks of the beauties of nature. If the ordinary mortal turns to art he looks for illustrations and reminders of what he likes in life. His ideal of art is the picture post card, or the magazine cover, because it

[1] Cf. Clive Bell and Roger Fry.

abides by his reality and suggests nothing he has not already discovered for himself. This is heresy to men who see in art, in each art, in every work of art, a new world with a light that never was, and who emerge from the aesthetic experience reborn.

For the hyper-aesthete, art is so different from anything else that to express the difference no terms can be too extravagant. His fervor is that of conviction, he has an enviable familiarity with art and knows whereof he speaks. Being human he shares the grosser experience of other men, but few of his fellows are connoisseurs of art. The aesthete is like a traveler telling the wonders of a far land; he is like a mystic or a lover trying to describe his experience.

It is rash for a man to deny that anyone else could have had an experience different from his: to deny all scenes not beheld with his own eyes, all sounds not heard with his own ears, all meanings not received by his reason; though ignorance has a way of claiming to be knowledge. It is hard to take a broad view with a narrow mind, or to base a true judgment on prejudice, and it may be prejudice to believe that the world is all of a piece, that there is nothing in it not already known in one's own bailiwick. Perhaps there is nothing in the nature of things to keep art from being as different from ordinary life as the aesthete says it is.

But the scientist approaching art must assume that it is part of the common world, that it can be treated in common with other human interests and activities. The scientist cannot admit a breach in nature through which superstitions and supernatural possibilities would pour in to swamp his hard-won achievements. He must assume that the artist is a man like other men, with the same body and the same mind, feeling heat and cold and hunger and all the passions. His materials must be those of this earth, his themes those of this life. What else could he work with? What else could he express? There is not, there must not be a mystery here, or science is lost.

Yet art is mysterious, because its essential quality, its originality and difference defy analysis. Since art can be felt and enjoyed but not measured or weighed, science cannot touch it except externally. If art were only what can be stated scientifically about it, the unique value of art would be lost. The mystic says the same of his experience: only the outside of it can be observed; the inner feeling cannot be penetrated by the psychologist; the mystic himself can hardly tell what that is, and that is the whole thing. The lover is equally dissatisfied with any scientific account of his experience, which would not be the intimate thing it is if anyone but the beloved could share it with him. The traveler also treasures the memory of things that no one could appreciate who had not seen them with the same eyes.

The beauty of art is that through it these precious inner things can after all be expressed — not communicated in the shorthand of conversation or the abstractions of science — but suggested by living symbols that give the feeling of the mystic ecstasy, the amorous intimacy, the atmosphere of an unknown country. The artist can take the very quality of an experience and whisper it like a secret in the heart.

To the aesthete the idea of approaching art naturalistically, in terms of " the live creature in the environment," is a four-footed notion grotesquely incompatible with the artistic consciousness, which develops not so much in give and take with actuality as in withdrawal to a room of one's own fancy. The scientist would say that nature joins together the beast of the field and the artist in his attic; the aesthete would answer that eons of evolution separate them. Both are right. The artist and his activity are part of nature; but a very special part. The ivory tower is built on the rock of reality, but it is a tower, and is of ivory.

One may trace a work of art back to the time and place that brought it forth; one may see its debt to the life around it; but the aesthete cares about its unique flowering rather than its universal roots. The model was there, the material and the suggestion were there; everything was there but the new synthesis, the creation that is the work of art itself. From the scientific point of view, bent upon seeing each thing in a setting that will explain it, to say that art is altogether different from other things is absurd; and the scientific investigator of art tries to put it back in the place from which aesthetes and artists have exalted it. He explains art as the natural product of the human creature in interaction with environment. He explains everything but the fact that art gives a new version of the old elements, with a quality that cannot be described, that can only be experienced.

In admitting this the scientist almost enters the ivory tower himself. He cannot accept the absolute separation of art from life; but in his own terms he seems to be stating what aesthetes are insisting when he says, with Dewey: "Aesthetic effect is due to art's unique transcript of the energy of the things of the world" (*Art as Experience*, p. 185). The scientific standpoint threatens to destroy the notion that art is holy ground entitled to special respect. The man of science says that art is a transcript of something already there; but the honest scientist, in admitting the uniqueness of the transcription, grants everything that the most jealous art-lovers should demand. If setting art apart from life is their way of expressing the uniqueness of art, to confess its uniqueness after showing all that it owes to the rest of experience is not less to honor art.

But while he is warped around close to the aesthete's position the scientist will add, after agreeing that art is something special, that it differs from ordinary experience not by constituting an escape from natural desire and feeling, not by holding the organism in abeyance and blotting out the environment, but by satisfying desire and arousing emotion more fully, by exercising the organism more completely and integrating it with nature more happily. Art then is not an alternative to life but a means of living more vividly.

Every phase of experience has a rational aspect which is like a handle for the scientist to grasp, and an irrational facet which he cannot grip except indirectly. But what slips from science adheres to art. The artist is not so much building up a world different from that of science as presenting another strain in the one world there is. No scientific advance will abolish the ineffability of immediate experience, of direct enjoyment and suffering. Science can more or less get at the conditions underlying what is experienced, and to some extent control them; science can change the face of the earth and the landscape of the mind: but what it feels like to live by grace of, or in spite of, scientific discovery; what is the emotion of riding in automobiles, using the telephone, or watching the waves; what is the meaning of work and play provided, or not yet destroyed, by technology; what is the significance of the contacts and conflicts possible or inevitable in modern civilization; what are the values appearing and disappearing or enduring — for all this we turn to art. Science is a powerful tool, but for appraisal of its fitness or lack of relevance we must rely on art, which alone can express what is immediate or ultimate. Science is an armory of ways and means; art is the arsenal of meaning.

The life-enhancing function of art is not so clear in our civilization as in the culture of primitive races and non-industrial societies, where art is more a communal affair in which everyone takes part easily and naturally, singing and dancing and carrying on traditional crafts. Nature-peoples appear to live with more eagerness and zest; though it may be romantic to believe that they are more wistful or more graceful in transmuting suffering through expression. Our industrial life is oppressive and dulling; it inculcates hardness and apathy both in success and failure. Wholesome joy and gentle sadness are rare in the absence of basic adjustment. Appreciative sensibility is too severely punished by our emotional climate to flourish, except in a few individuals who are thrust out from the shelter of callousness to endure, in the midst of other people, a peculiar ostracism relieved by secret delights.

What most men in our civilization ask of what they call art is a stimulant or sedative to enable them to withstand the harshness of daily living. Even persons who denounce artificiality in aestheticism are forced to think of art as escape and compensation, if not as a source of strength for a more strenuous participation in actuality. The aesthete seeks in art the opposite of what surrounds him, but is driven farther afield than other men because he abhors the ordinary retreats from reality where even art is infected with the banality he wants to avoid.

There is always an element of transcendence in art, but art tends to be more satisfying when felt as a fulfillment than as a repudiation of life; and life enhanced by art is happier than unaesthetic existence further impoverished by invidious comparison with art. An aesthete in our society cannot have the attitude of an Indian in rural Mexico, but may envy his artistic appreciation and ability and marvel at his freedom from affectation. There seems to be no dualism between art and life when works of art are made as articles of daily use and when their design is the rhythm of a healthy organism flowing spontaneously into all that is done. A day which is not a fiesta for the Mexican Indian will be the day after or the day before. Fiestas are not departures from everyday so much as celebrations of it, glorifying it, filling it with an undying throb and flicker. There are craftsmen in Mexico more creative than the rest, there are leaders in the dancing and the drama, but everyone helps in making the decorations and firecrackers, everyone shares in the fun. No one is left out because he has no money, no one stays at home because he is not invited, or because he is too busy, or because his aesthetic education has been neglected. Everyone is a spectator and everyone participates.

Whether it is possible to achieve in our industrial civilization a life as human and harmonious as that still enjoyed by much of Mexico in spite of poverty and violence, remains to be seen. But in Europe and the United States an artist or lover of beauty cannot feel at ease in the common life except as it is distilled in art, an art usually inaccessible to other people, largely on account of economic moats; and no one deplores more than the artist or aesthete the rift between life as it is lived and as it would be loved. Utopia, in contrast to actuality, has a value that might disappear with the contrast, and to imagine the realization of any social ideal may be no more fantastic than to suppose life suffused with the enchantment of a Byzantine mosaic or a Beethoven symphony. It is futile to compare reality and dream, but our society may suffer in comparison with the actual existence of men in the past and with the lot of many contemporaries. The mass of our fellow citizens are uprooted from participation in human values and the secure place in the community that have for ages characterized the state of nature for men whom we call uncivilized, a state yet more or less enjoyed by people who have not been corrupted and exploited by inroads of our civilization. In our present society most men are not only cut off from the integration and completeness their ancestors knew, but are deprived of the refinements of the aesthete as much as they are denied the satisfactions of a Mexican Indian.

For Dewey, unjust social divisions are to blame for the monopoly of art on the part of a few, rather than anything in the nature of art itself. The aesthete might answer that the kind of culture he values is necessarily a function of social inequality; and he might feel that the raptures of a few art-lovers are worth the toil and misery of the masses. But he might prefer to say that the only redeeming feature in our civilization is the enjoyment of art, inhumanly restricted as it is. The fine arts may not promise as much to the masses as the arts of social planning, but as long as these are unable to remove miserable living conditions, it is something that their ugliness should at least be transformed on canvas and in imagination. The aesthete cannot be blamed for his taste, or his alienation from people who do not share it, since he, as well as the man in the street, is a product of the civilization which has produced most of the art we admire if we profess to be cultured. From antiquity this civilization has rested upon conditions that have prevented most men from aspiring to culture at all. The Parthenon and the Pantheon arose upon the assumption that most men are slaves, a prejudice that has not disappeared after centuries of Christianity, despite declarations of independence and of the rights of man.

Wage slaves are not expected to appreciate the art of artists and aesthetes, and yet much of it has been the work of humble, obscure men, who won a distinction so difficult to win that we call them geniuses. What can we say when art issues from the depths of Africa or backward Mexico to catch the breath of persons who assume that the mass of men are incapable of aesthetic experience? What shall we say of the amazing art produced by civilized children when they are given the right stimuli and freed from inhibitions? Often education and sophistication seem to be an obstacle to art, and at least one kind of artist is a being who somehow retains the freshness of an unspoiled child or a primitive man. John Dewey is partially right that the artist is a person who keeps the alertness of the animal in his natural habitat.

But the art of the Mexican Indian may fail to move an average aesthete deeply despite a faultless sense of design and infallible power of execution. Because its representative content is remote and enigmatic to him this art appears to be largely a matter of abstract form, and it is hard even for an aesthete to be content with mere curves and colors, however lovely. Also the Indian's art is applied to objects of use; his designs rest on the needs of daily and religious life, or the fun of the fiesta. To appreciate his art as the Indian does, one should share his culture; to regard his patterns purely as abstractions is to miss their spirit. When our aesthetes fill in his forms with thoughts and feelings of their own the resulting literary impression is likely to satisfy them more than his most perfect works in themselves. Unless people of our background have unusual skill and patience in surrendering their sensibility to that of the Indian, they tend to enjoy his finest expression as an illustration of the kind of interpretation that D. H. Lawrence would give, or René d'Harnoncourt. For people like us, even with some aesthetic cultivation, Indian art borrows interest from what such men say; and when they endeavor to lead us into the experience of the Indian they fail as much as they succeed, for they must interpret him to us in terms that fit us rather than him.

No race has a monopoly of beauty, and no group, not even that of aesthetes and artists. But in this transitional period of Western civilization, to become aware of beauty is to love it with a passion almost illicit, with an intensity that is morbid, in contrast to the open-air affection possible in conditions more favorable to aesthetic experience, an intensity touched with fever. Beauty is tainted in this air, yet is one of the purest things there are; art is contaminated with an odor of immorality but is among the most moral of employments, demands severe sacrifice and is evidence of effort in pursuit of the ideal; the artist is often unhealthy and a little mad in this atmosphere, yet may be the sanest of men by a more human standard. Without him the sense of beauty might perish and health become a hollow thing, happiness a void.

Beauty is strewn wherever it is found. Art is a device for focusing and intensifying beauty, but it is already there, and sometimes to perfection, without the aid of art. Anything delightful in itself has beauty: to look at, or listen to, or think about. Perhaps it is best not to explain this delight, but simply to enjoy it, though an explanation can be given in one word: form. A definition is bound to be circular, but it may have a radius sufficient to be enlightening. Beauty is form: form is design or pattern; design is relatedness; and relatedness makes the delight that is the basis of beauty.

Art can provide a new experience, of materials in rhythms and harmonies which never existed before, and that never would exist outside art. It is this power of art that is missed by those who seek in pictures only the objects of everyday, who listen to music only for hints of the world beyond the concert hall. Familiar shapes and relationships occur in the most abstract art, but transposed and purified; and to look in art only for illustrations of life is to ignore the medium, the fact that a painted scene differs from an actual landscape in being painted. It is important to appreciate art as such, instead of using it only as a mirror or a sounding board; although a full appreciation includes, along with what is actually presented in art, an awareness of what adheres to it through the associations of the beholder.

The ivory tower aesthete is right in dismissing the " beauties of nature " so far as they are formless and owe their attraction to sheer physical refreshment; but wrong in so far as nature presents relationships that can be appreciated as if they were the result of art. And the ordinary mortal, who finds in art nothing but reminders of what he likes in life, is right in as much as art is a restatement of what is already there in common experience; but wrong if he perceives in art only what was obvious without it and misses the intensification, the heightening and tightening of formal relations peculiar to art. The man of scientific temper as well is entirely justified in emphasizing the basis of art in life, but shortsighted if he underestimates the towering of art above its foundation.

Forms created by the artist are not only diverting, they hide the human predicament and overcome it. Artistic form is a refuge for the human spirit, a haven from the inchoate and the inane. Man's mortal enemy, lurking behind all the evils that beset him, is the formless; and his one salvation, shining through all kinds of grace, is form. He would be homeless in any heaven without form, and with it he is anywhere at home. He must eat and mate; but, hungry and lonely or filled and beloved, as a human being form is his food and his affinity. Form is the manna of imagination; and nothing else matters because nothing better can be imagined. Wherever fate carries the ark of humanity on the flood of formlessness, all known forms are safe in the hold of the mind; and the only resting-place ever to be hoped for in the midst of the flood is the Ararat of art.

The darkest nights of the soul come when old forms die and new ones are not yet born, when faiths give way and mythologies collapse; temples are ruined, statues are broken and buried, paintings crack and fade, books and languages are lost. The old, when recovered, is often better than the new, and always better than nothing — the yawning alternative that can be stopped only with novelty grafted on the old and brought afresh into being by the creative power of art. Form is the stay of the spirit, whether stained with antiquity or new as the morning; because conscious life, which alone is human, is constituted by awareness of relations, by enjoyment of motives and themes, by love of ideas and dialectic, by passion for symphonies and philosophy; an awareness that is too easily missed even in youth, and that would be as hard to find as the fountain of youth if not for the magic of art.

In any field, from biography to astronomy, an artistic treatment is never displaced except by one that is more artistic. Myths give way only to more comprehensive and complex myths, though primitive beliefs hold their own among people who prefer naïve patterns. All man's works are works of art, or should be, in the sense of shaping material into satisfying form; and toil in which men cannot feel creative is always irksome. Soldiering and sailoring are not regarded as creative, but are attractive occupations on account of their rhythmic character, their style and their flourishes; but too often the forms and rhythms of work delight only an artist or an aesthete looking on.

If daily living could be made lovely for everyone, the so-called fine arts might lose their value, but that remains to be seen in the millennium. Meantime the isolated harmonies achieved by artists are not only a consolation for a few, but a goal for all human striving — a goal hidden from those who are thoughtless and insensitive, but dawning even on them as they become aware of values, and perhaps art alone can make them aware. Art is an earnest of the ideal, an indication and assurance of what may be hoped for; art is the great awakener and promiser; and now, as in the past, art fills the cup of an appreciative person to overflowing — momentarily, it may be, but one should not ask too much.

No matter how exact the information we acquire about a person, short of knowing him intimately, we lack the artist's revelation of him. The same is true of a people or a period, and even our own experience may come to life for us only when recreated by art. While art may romanticize a subject, a misrepresentation with a rhythmic rightness may be more convincing than a leaden fidelity, for no one believes the truth is lame. A scientist worth his salt will dance around the facts until they join hands with him and move as if to numbers. All the ultimate canons of science and life are aesthetic, because men must have unity despite variety, and order even in progress, no matter how much faith it takes. They will hear harmony behind every discord, and if there is no music of the spheres — there ought to be.

If all existence could be made aesthetic we should not need music, painting and literature for escape or compensation; but we might crave them more than ever, with a deeper appreciation, as a further refinement and fulfillment of our lives. If we all had beautiful homes, clothing and cities, and were ourselves lovely, we might no longer enjoy some of the art that has been admired in the past; but we should still appreciate the formal qualities of Greek statues and temples, of Byzantine mosaics and Gothic cathedrals. However ideal our existence may become, as long as it is touched with love and edged by death we shall respond to the tragic poets. We shall feel that whatever knowledge they lack, they know enough in showing what it is to live and love and die.

FORM IN ART AND LIFE

The long controversy as to the relative importance of form and significant content in art is still going on. Formalists hold that to allow any value to association is sentimental, while their opponents assert that to confine aesthetic appreciation to form alone is to freeze real feeling out of the experience. Informalists respond to the meanings which transcend a work of art rather than to the perfection that a craftsman has skilfully introduced into it as a physical object. They use art as a take-off for a flight of imagination instead of as a perch to alight on and cling to. They frankly prefer to a work of art without associations for them a relatively formless one that will serve as a souvenir.

There have been persons who found beauty only in arabesques without meaning or in music without words; there have been those indifferent to any intrinsic worth in pattern or design, who appreciated form only as a base for association; and there have been persons who were responsive both to the way a work of art is articulated and to how it refers to life, how it interprets experience, how it comments on the strange lot of being human, how it asks the old questions, awakes the old wonder and gives a heightened sense of mystery for an answer. Some people have believed that form and feeling are the same, that form and matter, form and content, are one; that the essence of art is to overcome the oppositions of reason and sense, of freedom and necessity, the infinite and the finite. But no one has maintained that artistic form is simply the rhythm of reminiscence, that the process of association is altogether formal.

It may sound absurdly paradoxical to say that the apparent aimlessness of reverie and the supposed firm control of artistic arrangement are as much alike as the two sides of a shield; that instead of one being opposed to the other, or molded to the other, one is the obverse and the other the reverse of the same thing. Yet such seems to be the case as soon as one gives up the untenable idea that there is anything arbitrary or artificial about the form of a genuine work of art, or that there is any lack of design in associational patterns.

When the essence of art is felt to be its architectonic, any inclusion of life experience is likely to be regarded as irrelevant or superfluous; or, if valued, to be looked upon as an added merit, a lucky increment, not necessarily to be expected in a work of art. When, on the contrary, expression is assumed to be the important thing the apparent absence of form is condoned, or the presence of it is not the chief reason for rejoicing. As long as form and expression are thought of as belonging to different orders, no matter how they blend, the question will still arise as to whether art would not be more artistic in foregoing even the most intimate union with any meaning that transcends immediate, objective form. But question of the fitness of adding representative content to form disappears if it is seen that such content is formal. The formalist is like the man who goes to church for the ritual and may or may not care about the sermon; the associationist is like the person who goes

for a message to illuminate actual living, and inciden-
tally, if at all, for the liturgy.   To insist that form and
expression are inseparable is like believing that the sermon should coalesce with the rest of the service.

But in the case of art in the highest (and also in the
lowest, as long as it is art) there is no point in holding
that sermon and service should be unified, because they
are indissoluble.   Not the real form, but only the skeleton of it, can be lifted out of a work of art; not the real
meaning, but only the ghost of it, can be separated from
the form.   If this is not true all the tomes of aesthetics
have been written in vain; if this is not true the aesthetic
experience is an illusion.

Yet even the skeleton of form is significant of its nature.   Whatever else it is, form is repetition.   Form is
a picket fence which delights a boy slapping a stick along
it; form is the beat of a drum, the click of castanets, the
sliding feet of dancers, the jingle of rhyme and the style
of Gertrude Stein.   A rose is a rose is a rose.

The repetitious quality characterizing aesthetic experience is most evident, perhaps, in the temporal arts
of music and the dance, literature and drama.   A musical or literary composition supplies its own past as it
develops, so that when it is well under way it can hark
back to earlier stages with an effect as telling as if it were
carrying us back to the scenes of our childhood.   It is
the imaginative sense of time that counts.   Within the
dream-time of a work of art a fraction of an actual day
is enough to yield all the fullness of three score years
and ten.   The very meaning of music is to be a composition, to be all of a piece, to develop and vary what is
given in the beginning and come to a close with a
final summation of repetition.   Even a single sound is

a complex affair, and one sound does not make a melody. For that there must be a succession of sounds; and the succession must be agreeable, which means that the tones will be felt to follow as parts of the same whole. But a pleasant tune does not constitute an opera or a symphony. For that, more than one element, melodic, harmonic or rhythmic, must be developed with variations into a theme, and themes must follow and recall each other in a comprehensive composition.

In order to return one must have gone forward some distance, but even the " static " arts enable attention to move on to new ideas before slipping back to the old and familiar. Beauty involves form, and form requires space and time or space-time. Confined to a mathematical point or instant, form would cease to exist, for to be itself it must have scope to range about and become an arrangement, must have leisure to repeat itself into a pattern. In the symmetry of paintings, whether the balance is obvious or subtle, what is on the right of the fulcrum is repeated by something on the left, something which, however different, is psychically the same. Repetition in a painting goes on up and down and diagonally, as well as sideways, and in a swirl. The repetition entails color, line, light, dark, mass — all the elements to be distinguished as part of a painting. The Odyssey of one color can be followed all over a canvas: a splash here, a streak there; it will appear within other colors and even in the shadows, until the whole surface is suffused with it. But always the same color will be different in a good painting; even the tiniest area will ripple into varied shades and tints.

Sculpture is less clearly mnemonic, but here too return and repetition are still the essence of the matter. In a frieze there is no doubt of this, or wherever sculpture is accessory to architecture. But even in a single plastic figure there can be any amount of interweaving reference among surfaces and volumes. The beauty of any style of architecture inheres in the way the units echo and swell and sustain one another, in doors and windows, horizontals and verticals, surfaces and volumes, and all details. Throughout there are oppositions, but these are repeated as well as the parallel tendencies, and all participate in a grand reiteration of a central unity.

The foundation of form and the source of aesthetic experience is not mechanical but vital repetition. Merely to harp in the same way on the same thing spells monotony and boredom, because to strike again and again with the same emphasis on the same note is not enough. The boy with his stick speeds up and slows down in his progress along the picket fence; he presses harder or not so hard; he skips and syncopates the beats, like a drummer or a girl with castanets or a blacksmith with his hammer. It is doubtful whether a human being would ever maintain a regular beat except in attendance upon a machine; and no one expects a musician to keep time like a metronome. In fact, to hear the ticking of a clock or the dripping of water is unbearably tedious unless it slips from attention or is unconsciously accommodated to the pulse of one's own organism, so that the tick becomes tick-tock, the drip a drippety drip, drip drip.

Artistic or vital repetition is a process of inoculating with sameness such a variety of elements that the result, instead of being a host of identical nonentities, will be a company of individuals joined in a secret bond, all alive with their own life but fired with the same fever. It does not matter how many rules or conventions of or-

ganization are obeyed or defied, whether the units march
in close formation or break their ranks in seeming rout,
if, as in response to a signal, they return to the attack
before it is too late and vindicate their discipline by a
common loyalty.

If repetition is of first importance in artistic form, variation is second. Variation must be subsidiary to repetition because in every kind of art, exciting as a shift may
be, the introduction of novelty never has the emotional
impact of a return to familiarity; indeed, novelty is not
welcome at all unless it turns out to be a sheep in wolf's
clothing and can be brought back into the fold. Form
cannot assimilate something new except as a variation of
what is already there; and to be a variation of something
else is to be more or less a repetition of it. In a work
of art the whole is repeatedly present throughout the
parts. Art is a creative advance making possible a creative repetition and recapitulation, for from the beginning, through a series of partial recurrences and new
departures, each work of art longs for a triumphal return
that will be final.

This turns out to be true even in the case of composi-
tions and buildings where at first glance it is not so, or
else they are not felt to be artistic. The matter is complicated and made interesting by the fact that where the
repetition of a feature is expected, that feature can be
suggested so as to be felt even though absent, as when
the boy deliberately skips a picket in the fence. He may
omit several pickets in succession and still resume the
rhythm, because the unstressed beats count anyhow in
his organism. In music a number of quick notes will be
equivalent to one long one, a deliberate discord may
enhance a harmony, and a resolution be completed with-

out a return to the tonic. In poetry the rhymes, as they vary, keep bringing home the same rhyme scheme; the meter, through established or *de novo* deviations, remains a firm foundation. In prose also there is a kind of rhythmic recurrence; and in all literature an attitude or atmosphere will be sustained; there will be a continuity of diction and imagery; there will be a pervasive tone or quality that is called style.

Recurrence and confluence are more conspicuous in an extensive work like a symphony or a building than in a thing like a small vase, a coin or a piece of jewelry; but there may be amazing intricacy in miniature, as there can be a tempest in a teapot. Even when the simplicity of an ornament or a stuff seems innocent of complication, of any effort to lure the attention from point to point through a design of recurrent and cumulative effect, there is nevertheless enough differentiation to induce a circulation of interest, however gentle; there is room for a bit of roaming and returning, or the object is not an *objet d'art*. The sheen of a fabric, or the luster of a precious stone, is the most concentrated kind of beauty, but is ample enough for undulation, shaped enough for a play of light. Like marble in a mosque the smallest surface of the aesthetic experience is veined with variety and polished with oneness; or, like Syrian silk, it is woven of identity and ribbed with difference. The stab of beauty may be very sudden but the blade is damaskeened.

The most beautiful trees are often not the straight ones but those which have been twisted by the wind, and have braced themselves by a counterpoint of trunk and branches only to be again forced over, until at last a majestic, spreading balance is attained, like that of a great poem. Even the beauty of a straight tree is

largely in its lack of straightness, the tapering of the
stem, the progression and alternation of the boughs, and
the gentle swaying of the whole, with an effect that in-
creases in a row of trees against the horizon. But alone,
or in a grove, nothing contributes to the charm of trees
more than the feeling that their dignity is human, that
in the long watch they keep through the years they are
companions of ours, repeating in a silent variation our
own experience, and perhaps giving us a good example.
This is especially true of familiar trees that were growing there when we were growing up, and are standing
yet, in spite of change: landmarks of memory.

The repetition which makes a thing beautiful does not
take place entirely within the thing itself, but is also a
function of one's repeated relationship with it. The
form beheld in a work is enriched by the in-weaving of
patterns from the beholder's experience — explicitly,
when he is aware that his associations are entering in;
implicitly, when he seems to be wholly absorbed in the
inherent form of the object itself, without knowingly
importing anything into it. One imports something into
every object of attention; no perception is entirely passive; and the more interesting a thing is, the more it appeals, the more certain one is to meet it half way. A
work of art beseeches for assistance, for sympathy and
appreciation. It is never complete in itself, and nothing
can complete it but the response of an appreciator. The
physical thing called a work of art is only a few stimuli,
a framework of hints and cues. When most ambitious
it is just a beginning.

Every symphony is unfinished and would remain so
if the audience only soaked it up in a soundless sponge
of flesh. Nothing would be gained if the audience

echoed like brass or reverberated with the voice of a thousand amplifiers; nothing would be added if hearing were like the most delicate phonograph recording, missing no nuance, and able to repeat a whole composition forever and ever. There would be no music at all if not for the sympathetic vibration of an appreciative response, the only genuine resonance. What vibrates in appreciation is not just the tympanum of the ear but the strings of the heart; not merely the instruments of the orchestra, but the thumping drums of memory and the faint flutes of the past.

This accounts for the aesthetic value an object may have for us when it has no particular form, or when its form apparently is not what endears it to us. The moon alone in the sky would not attract a painter seeking suggestion for a composition, yet might move us deeply through our associations with it and through the number of times we have read about it in poetry. Even when the moon is part of an inherently formal setting of trees, clouds and water, it may not be the intrinsic loveliness of the scene that explains our emotion, but the pattern of our fancy. So the beauty of a Persian rug or an inlaid table from Damascus may inhere not only in the immediate design, with its formal, stylized representation of the interrelations of experience; but the beauty will be enhanced by the subtle tracery of our impressions of the Orient.

One who has become conscious of a past is fascinated by the echoes of it in the present and anticipates the future as an opportunity for further reminiscence. Travel, without a store of associations to be stirred, is a fool's paradise, and life itself is a journey that is worth while only as it recalls steps taken long ago. Even children look forward to repetition of experiences they have had. They like to hear the same stories and to play the same games over and over, and will not allow alterations. We are all more or less like that. When we see a play for the second time we tend to dislike changes in the cast or setting, and the chief joy of friends is the fact of their continuing to be their old selves. An expansion of former experiences may be hoped for, but a rejection of them for something vastly different cannot be welcomed. Children dream of growing up, but as a continuation of what they have been doing, in play and imagination.

Stevenson, in one of his essays, tells how he liked to write his name in the front of every book he read, with the place and date, for a reminder in the future; and we all plan for a return over the way we have come. We take photographs and hang them on the wall or treasure them in albums. We keep journals or scrapbooks, and hate to throw things away, because we have learned how powerfully a relic will pull us back across the years. A souvenir is prized apart from its intrinsic merit, because its value derives from a receding realm that but for this vestige would be lost to view. An Aladdin's lamp, though it might look quaintly out of place in a modern apartment, would without apology be given a position of honor by anyone fortunate enough to own it. Yet everyone possesses such a lamp in cherishing mementos that, when touched or merely looked upon, evoke the past.

A foreign coin, a tramway ticket, a hotel bill in their very commonplaceness may bring back a trip as vividly as a handsome trophy. If we are honest with ourselves we must admit that we recall ships, trains and hotels with as much delight as museums, palaces and theaters we went abroad to see. Chance acquaintances met along the way, maids and waiters whose words and gestures we remember, beckon our backward glance as much as important people to whom we had introductions, or great actors and singers whom we made a point to hear. Whatever stirs recollection may take on aesthetic value; but also, whatever we are moved to remember tends to acquire the same value.

The keepsake is the key to aesthetic experience, and a work of art is like a collection of mementos. The ordinary reminder brings back a particular experience: art instils the wistfulness of all the souvenirs that anyone has ever had. But while we may derive from the contemplation of a tramway ticket, reminiscent of adventures in Europe, an aesthetic experience as real as could be vouchsafed us in beholding an ambitious work of art, there is a great difference between a bit of paper with a little printing on it, even in Italian, and a painting, a statue or a poem. The difference is that a trivial souvenir cannot be expected to arouse an aesthetic response in anyone but the person who treasures it, except through unusual sympathy; whereas a work of art moves many people and represents an appreciable amount of work toward that end.

Yet the most elaborate work of art has no charm for people who do not appreciate it, and it may remain a thing of beauty for one lone admirer. Colored canvas or chiseled marble is not metaphysically more lovely than a crumpled street car ticket; and the ticket, as well as they, may possibly become the cue for an aesthetic response. It is a mistake to limit the aesthetic experience to appreciation of technique, when a thing manifesting very little skill, or a natural object embodying none at all, may give as deep an emotion of beauty as a masterpiece of art.

The artist himself may deliberately enlarge the form of his work by attempting to enlist and control the appreciator's associations. The literary artist almost always does this, for he cannot help foreseeing much of the imagery his words will evoke; and painters depend directly upon the experience of their public in planning many of their effects. Composers also are prone to transcend the abstractness of music by any device that will cause further reverberation in the labyrinth of the hearer's breast.

The opera, the oratorio, and all songs assume that sentimental association and musical structure can be combined. Respighi, realizing that associations are simply an expansion of artistic form, in his tone poem on *The Pines of Rome* does not confine himself to composing for the orchestra, but through notes in the program appeals to the audience to refresh their memory or imagination of Rome. This would shock an advocate of pure music, and would be inartistic if the composer's effort to move people through the program conflicted with his effect on them through the orchestra; but Respighi is justified in so far as the associations he calls out through the program reinforce the form of his work.

What first attracts us to a work may be a superficial affinity between it and our own life: it may recall a childhood scene through what it represents, or it may simply have been in the house when we were young. In that case our affection for it would be called sentimental, would be said to have nothing to do with the skill of the artist and the quality of his spirit, or with the material object itself. The situation seems to be altogether different when we become attached to something because it is inherently artistic, something perhaps unknown to us until recently. In the first case our interest seems to be independent of form; in the second our interest may seemingly be aroused solely by the form the object actually has.

The form which an artist has built into a work may be more charged with the rhythms of human fate than the complex of associations which the owner of the work can inject into it, but it would be hard to say. We may say that the built-in form will stand longer and appeal to more people than the web of relations added by the owner and invisible to others. If one man's memories are as formal in their pattern as another's, then the associational factor would seem to cancel out and leave the intrinsic structure of the work to stand or fall alone. But this in-itselfness of a work never can be extricated from that which each appreciator brings to it from his own life.

The danger of taking this position is that it threatens to wipe out any distinction between being appreciative and being sentimental. The safeguard lies in equating appreciation with self-conscious awareness, and identifying sentimentalism with a superficial, uncritical enthusiasm. A person who picks up the conventional remarks about form and composition and cannot see the experiential, organic, vital basis of form, is no less sentimental than a person who approaches a painting as he would a comic strip, on the lookout only for the clichés of human behavior. Sentiment can be very sophisticated: it may rest upon very intricate and highly formal relations. And formalism can be very unsophisticated: it may rest on nothing but abstraction and the absence of sentiment.

Form is an arrangement of pleasing repetition; and the associations aroused by art, or implanted in art, instead of being radically different from its objective structure, are an extension of it. The difference between a design presented in the sensuous stuff of art, and the same thing embellished with memories, is like that between a piece of music played on one instrument and swelled by a whole orchestra. Life itself seems to have the kind of organic pattern that characterizes artistic form; and form in art might have no interest for us if it did not clarify and focus the formal character of life. When we like a painting for the way it is painted we may not be having an experience vastly different from liking a painting because it recalls the past. In art, as in life, one enjoys nostalgia. A work of art stirs the beholder to reminiscence, both by transcending its immediate boundaries and by inducing an artificial retrospect within them. One cannot say that inherent beauty alone is formal and set it over against adherent beauty, because what is often scorned as sentimental reverie, throughout its associations, may retain over a greater surface the same relations as the inherent form of the art object itself, as the circles which spread outward from a pebble flung into a pool keep their shape until they reach the utmost edge.

Repetition and recognition, which are the essence of form in art, are also the quintessence of the meaning the formalist would exclude from art. No experience is more purely formal than that of going back to visit an old friend, being delighted to find him the same and being surprised by variations on himself which, while

they are perfectly in character, are so vital in their spon-
taneity that they could not have been foreseen. When
one returns in fact or fancy to an old haunt there is the
same recognition of the familiar, the same interest in the
elements of novelty which have emerged to vary the old
theme that one experiences in enjoying the "purest"
music. Thus, when a work of art stimulates a train of
imaginative return, artistic form is not impugned; form
is not required to vie with something antithetic to form,
or to blend miraculously with its opposite. Instead,
form is enriched through further form. Variations of
material and technique will distinguish one work of art
from another, as dissimilar experiences will prevent any
two men from having the same memories; but schemati-
cally, all works of art and all reminiscences will be alike.

The difference between enjoyment of retrospection
and appreciation of structure within a work of art is that
in art the repetition is planned on purpose to give the
experience of recognition, whereas life seems to flow on
its way beyond our control and heedless of aesthetic
effect; and if we can control destiny we rarely do so
with the idea of planning artistic recapitulations. Yet
even the most unpremeditated experience shapes into
patterns aesthetic in retrospect. The conditions of existence, the limitations necessarily imposed on anything
by the fact of being itself, provide everywhere for the
meditative eye designs as definite as those of snow crystals, and as infinitely various as life can always be within
its possibilities.

But while life spontaneously flows into molds, human
beings continually strive to impose more form than life
would exhibit without their effort. They devote a surprising amount of energy and ingenuity to stylizing their

experience — partly to forge ahead more vigorously, but also to achieve the aesthetic satisfaction of integration and equilibrium. Men need to think that history repeats itself. Even when overwhelmed by fate they are comforted to think that it is fate which overcomes them, or the laws of nature, or the inscrutable will of God, as was foretold, as was written, as was ordained from everlasting to everlasting. Recurring ceremonies, with a rhythm like that of the revolving seasons, give men the sense that life is proceeding on even keel, through storm and calm, homeward bound. Religion gives comfort and peace in many ways, but always through repetition. The traditional is sacred. It is unsettling to experiment with new forms, almost a contradiction, since forms are essentially conservative and repetitious, reliable because they are ancient. The novel is strange and dangerous. Only the old can be holy. So religion pours her new wine into old bottles. She advances reluctantly and would rather be turned to a pillar of salt than not look back.

To have a real return one must really go away, and the farther one wanders without forfeiting a homecoming, the more glorious a return one may expect. It is an old story that people seek beauty everywhere only to find it most truly when they come home. The fatted calf of the aesthetic experience is fed by the waywardness of the prodigal, and life makes prodigals of us all, whether we have the *Wanderlust* or not. Unavoidably we drift away from where we were, if we do not actually strive for something ever beyond; but inevitably, whatever carries us on, we are drawn back with a wonderful sense of completion, back to where we were — with the difference that during our absence we have changed, as well as the place we left, so that the more complete the return the more tragically aware we must be of the abyss between the present and the past. Art, and especially great art, for all the joy it may contain will make us wistful, because art evokes the past and no one can be reminiscent without emotion. The characteristic of the aesthetic fact is not merely pleasure but the pang of recognition.

An experience may at the very first be definitely pleasant or unpleasant, but the aesthetic quality proper emerges only in repetition. An experience must have been very disagreeable if it is unpleasant to recall it, because, if possible, our minds manage subconsciously to reinterpret an unhappy event so that the memory of it is not painful. We naturally want to renew our pleasures and avoid our pains, but regardless of whether we wish to repeat an experience or not, if it is repeated an aesthetic value tends to supervene, because repetition is the basis of form.

It may be objected that the important thing in aesthetic experience is not so much the sense of pastness as the presence of rich configuration. But since new experience is always slight compared to the vastness of the old, it is almost entirely in the past that configuration must be sought. A potentially rich object will not offer much when approached in isolation as a bare matter of fact, whereas the humblest detail assumes Homeric grandeur in the train of its antecedents. The deepest experience is always retrospective, because it is impossible all at once, in the first flush of a situation, to appreciate it fully. For Marcel Proust all value inheres in the remembrance of things past. In the moment of first experience, he says, we merely expose the negative of con-

sciousness and only later, at our leisure, can we develop
the significance of that moment. Hence for Proust the
essence of art is the expression of memory.

The richest beauty includes memories with their am-
plitude of configuration, and admiration for relics of
antiquity shows how far association alone can go toward
constituting aesthetic experience. The mutilated condition of many famous statues, and the patina on them,
faithfully imitated in good reproductions — indeed, any
evidence of age — becomes an integral part of aesthetic
charm. Beauty seems always to be increased by belonging to the past and becoming classic. We do not have
the most complicated response to anything contemporary unless it can lose its newness in seeming to be a return of former glamor, and when an artist impresses us
as great, it is often a shock to learn that he is still alive.
Usually it takes longer than a lifetime for an artist's
worth to be established, since artistic greatness is as much
reputation or reflection of past achievement as present
performance, just as beauty is adherent configuration as
well as intrinsic design. The new has no reverberation,
no legend, no aura of sacred names. Were it possible
to consider inherent form alone, without reference to
the patterns that cling about it, the new might more
often win the palm, but the old is rarely at a disadvan-
tage. When artists and sincere lovers of the beautiful
are modernistic they are prone to think they are being
classic or primitive, that they are escaping from some
unhallowed contemporary or recent aberration from an
old ideal. Certainly when the ordinary mortal wants
something beautiful his imagination carries him back,
perhaps not far, but far enough to find a model steeped
in sentiment for him. In his new house, with its mod-

ern conveniences, he will likely want windows of small leaded panes and a roof sway-backed as if with the weight of years. We move on, but facing backward, so that we do not appreciate novelty as it emerges, but only after it has coalesced with the familiar.

Thirst for novelty bespeaks an uncultivated, unaesthetic taste compared to joy in the mellowness of the old. Novelty-seeking seems callow and feverish to one who has sensed the inexhaustible heritage of the ages. Ahead is the adventure of the unknown, with no assurance of anything to justify the courage to push on. Boys and explorers may dream of planting a flag deep in the wilderness; they may for a while be satisfied with knowing that they have set foot where no one else has ever been. But pride in straying palls on men who are more than adventurers and who realize the increasing culture to be gained in recovery of the past. When men of vision look ahead they find themselves looking back — to Jesus, to Pericles, to some imagined youth of the race, if not to their own youth which soon recedes to the realm of imagination.

In the van of civilization we proceed blindly, lightened of all that we have left behind, and the faster we advance the drearier the waste ahead. But if we face about, every step to the rear brings an increment of meaning, for as much as the dead outnumber the living the past outweighs the present. Values which spontaneously arise even under pioneer conditions cannot adequately be appreciated without the perspective of tradition; and were our own day a veritable golden age we should not realize it unless we could survive to view it with the eyes of posterity. The past shimmers through a glory of associations, in contrast to the bare present.

Greece, Rome, the Middle Ages, the Renaissance: the very names are poetic; but our own time is waiting to be glossed by memory.

As the Romans went back to Greece, we go to Europe. We should develop our own culture, and slowly we shall, but meantime we must return. So far, a broader background than that of Europe seems superfluous, eccentric; and culture attempting to be universal is specious, because to be genuine it must be cherished. Culture is too volatile for exposure to all the winds that blow. Essentially aesthetic, it is distilled by repetition and will evaporate if not kept in the crystal phial of familiarity. The world is wide, and one part of it as old as another, but while it may be interesting to see Alaska and Australia, they do not have the pull of the past. It is an accident of tradition that some antiquities retain their hold upon us while some novelties soon acquire the attraction of age. We are aware of the antiquity of Egypt and are beginning to appreciate the archeology of Mexico, but impressive as their temples are they cannot equal the fascination of Europe for us, because they do not quite belong to what is for us the past.

Nothing can be cultural that does not become sufficiently part of our memories for us to emotionalize it. The classics are not culture if we have not loved them and lived with them enough to make them romantic. Even science becomes cultural to its devotees who are in love with it and fond of going over and over its structures — making discoveries, yet finding old friends in them. But a smattering of science hardly suffices to give a deep feeling, and for most of us science is too new to be cultural, too much in process to have the charm of things to which we return with emotion. Culture begins beyond the mere recollection of names, when names bring back the past.

This view need not ignore the zest of looking forward, because what one anticipates in aesthetic experience is repetition, either imaginative renewal of actual experience, or actual experience that will give imaginative return. One hesitates to undertake the appreciation of a new art form or to travel in a strange country unless one has been reading or hearing about it. Then to approach it means going back with the homing pigeons of imagination to a previous acquaintance. Even when it is the novel part of an experience that is awaited with pleasure, the desire is to repeat previous enjoyment of novelty, in so far as the aesthetic attitude is present. To get the old thrill we may have to seek it in new things, but new things will not delight us aesthetically unless they recall the old freshness, unless they renew our youth and enable us again to see the world glorious as on the first day.

Sometimes we have the sense of returning to a familiar position when we know that we could not have been there before. In such a case there may have been in our past a situation analogous to the present one; or the idea of it, suggested perhaps by art, may have remained in our minds like a bell to be struck. Often, on a trip, we feel our past forming, and we look ahead to the time when we shall look back to this moment, so that in the midst of actual experience it is like reliving it after many years. Especially in art the formal character of all experience comes to a focus. In the form of the art object is fixed the pattern of the artist's past; adhering to the object is the web of the appreciator's relations with it; and merging with it is the configuration of the appreciator's life, interwoven with a constellation of racial memories.

Like footprints in the sand, forms created by an artist are the impress of his personality, the evidence that he passed this way, with the whole weight of his being, with the stride that was his, in the direction of his destiny. After he has gone, by easy stages and forced marches, along the shore of oblivion, his tracks follow step by step, unable to overtake him but tireless in pursuit, until wiped out by the waves of time. In the shape of everything he does, and all along the path of his performance, the creative advance of the artist is repeated in his record. To appreciate his work is to recapitulate his life, not the irrelevancies of it but the essence.

The form of art is always flexible enough to fit the significant facts of the artist's life; and his life is always rhythmic enough to become pure form when expressed in art. Life is one thing after another, held together in memory, regardless of what the things are; and art is a repetition of elements synthesized in imagination. The difference is that only the person himself, if he knows himself, and those who know him well, can feel the coherence of his life; whereas the unity of the biography, when objectified in art, is so obvious that often it is played off against the life itself, as belonging to another order.

The arrangement of elements in a work of art is like the configuration of events in a person's life, because art is always the expression of life, and not only of the artist's own experience but of the human lot. A biographer or psychologist can find the correlation between an artist's performance and his existence, discrepant as they may seem; and a philosopher can see an artist's whole age in his work — or all the ages.

Some critics have marveled at Proust's ability to bring a formal structure out of his autobiographical material. But by his own admission the undeniable unity of his work forced itself upon him instead of being achieved by him. Wherever he picked up his reminiscing he was led from one point to another as if he were reading instead of writing great literature, except that it took infinitely more patience. His task was to retrace and reclaim all that his life had lapped against, by following out the interconnections in his past which familiarity with fine art helped him to see and express. To recover an experience and wrap it close within him he had only to see a relation between it and something already his own — a relation of similarity or difference, it did not matter. His *forte* was metaphor, which, to Aristotle, was the mark of genius.

The artist is a man who feels form in himself and life so keenly that to emphasize and celebrate form is for him the burden and the joy of living. The rhythms of his experience engage with the shapes he creates, and then mesh with the associational patterns of the appreciator who finally limits or unlimits the reach of the artist's work. The inherent beauty in the midst is no more formal than the beauty interlocking with it from the life of the artist and the life of the appreciator; and, like wheels within wheels, the movements of all three kinds of form are so geared together that no one can separate them, and no one should.

Return and repetition are fundamental to art as they are to life, and it is natural that life and art should reinforce each other since each is an extension of the other. When life has most the quality that makes it worth living it is most like a great work of art; and when art is most artistic it is most evocative of the deepest experience of a lifetime.